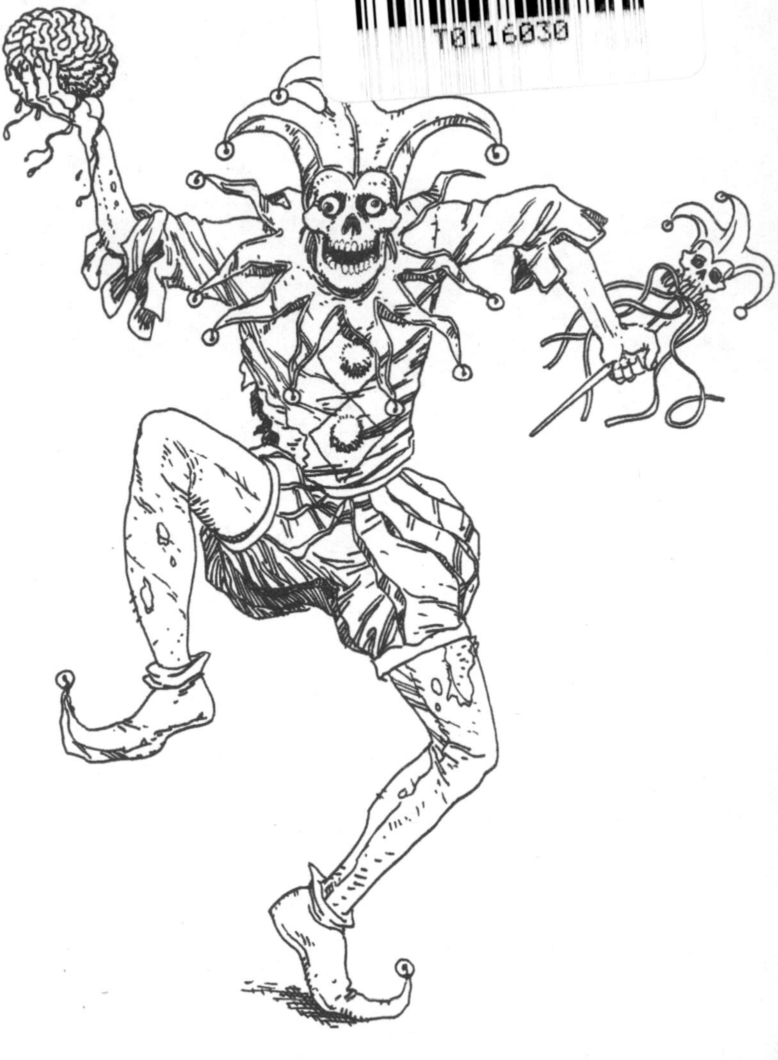

About the Author

MICHAEL P. SPRADLIN is the author of the *New York Times* bestseller *It's Beginning to Look a Lot Like Zombies!* and *Every Zombie Eats Somebody Sometime*, as well as several children's picture books, the novels and manga volumes in the Spy Goddess series, and the Youngest Templar novels. He lives in Michigan with his family.

About the Illustrator

JEFF WEIGEL is the illustrator of the *New York Times* bestseller *It's Beginning to Look a Lot Like Zombies!* and its sequel, *Every Zombie Eats Somebody Sometime*. He wrote, illustrated, and designed the children's picture books *Atomic Ace (He's Just My Dad)*, *Atomic Ace and the Robot Rampage*, and the historical graphic adventure novel *Thunder from the Sea*. He lives with his wife in Belleville, Illinois.

JACK
AND
JILL
Went Up to Kill

Also by Michael P. Spradlin and Jeff Weigel

Every Zombie Eats Somebody Sometime
It's Beginning to Look a Lot Like Zombies!

Also by Michael P. Spradlin

SPY GODDESS NOVELS
Live and Let Shop
To Hawaii, with Love

SPY GODDESS MANGA
The Chase for the Chalice
The Quest for the Lance

THE YOUNGEST TEMPLAR NOVELS
Keeper of the Grail
Trail of Fate
Orphan of Destiny

PICTURE BOOKS
The Legend of Blue Jacket
Texas Rangers: Legendary Lawmen
Daniel Boone's Great Escape
Off Like the Wind!: The First Ride of the Pony Express
Baseball from A to Z

JACK
AND
JILL

Went Up to Kill

A Book of Zombie Nursery Rhymes

Michael P. Spradlin

Illustrations by Jeff Weigel

HARPER

NEW YORK • LONDON • TORONTO • SYDNEY

HARPER

 For information, address HarperCollins Publishers, 195 Broadway, New York, NY 10007.

HarperCollins books may be purchased for educational, business, or sales promotional use. For information, please e-mail the Special Markets Department at SPsales@harpercollins.com.

FIRST EDITION

Illustrations by Jeff Weigel
Designed by Justin Dodd

ISBN 978-0-06-208359-3

15 OV/RRD 10 9 8 7 6 5 4 3 2

For my wife Kelly.
There's no one else I'd rather
spend a Zombie Apoclypse with.

CONTENTS

Author's Note: Mother Goose Was Really a Zombie.
  I'm Not Even Kidding.   xiii
There Was an Old Zombie Woman Who Lived in a Shoe   1
Little Jack Horner   3
A-Tisker, A-Tasker   5
Baa, Baa, Zombie Sheep   7
Zombie Willie Winkie   9
Zombiecat, Zombiecat   11
There Was an Undead Man   13
Humpty Dumpty   15
Sing a Song of Sixpence   17
Jack Sprat Was a Revenant   19
Jack and Jill Went Up to Kill   23
Little Miss Muffet Turned on a Tuffet   25
Do You Know the Undead Man?   27
Old King Cole Is a Merry Old Ghoul   29
The Monkey and the Weasel   31
The Owl and the Pussycat   35
Mother Goose   39
Mary, Mary, Quite Contrary   41
Hey! Diddle, Diddle!   43
Hickory, Dickory, Dock!   45
Zombie Simon   47
Jack Be Nimble   49

Little Bo Peep   51

Peter, Peter, Fresh Brain Eater   53

Three Zombie Kittens   55

Mary Ran from a Zombie Lamb   59

Little Boy Blue   61

The Zombie Queen of Hearts   63

Three Zombie Mice   65

MOTHER GOOSE WAS REALLY A ZOMBIE. I'M NOT EVEN KIDDING.

Throughout human history, the Zombie has held a prominent place in our literature. And the undead's contributions to our stories are perhaps no more prevalent than in the development of the nursery rhyme. Like the oldest tales, first spun by ancient storytellers around the campfire in the cave, our nursery rhymes were, at first, simple parables. Short lessons in morality, which furthered our evolution as a species.

And in many cases the nursery rhyme was a veritable instructional mantra on ridding our homes and neighborhoods of the dead come back to life. Scholars have clearly shown that nursery rhymes have been full of Zombie references for centuries. One only needs to think of monkeys and weasels getting their heads bashed in and the terrifying screams of Humpty Dumpty as he loses his broken head to a brain-eating troop of the king's men to understand that our ancestors were plagued by the Zombie menace for eons.

Obviously, as the years have passed and the Zombie menace has waxed and waned, these nursery rhymes were toned down so as to be palatable for children to hear, often before they drifted off in blissful slumber. But one need not dig very far to find the truth. These rhymes tell tales of horror and Zombie insurrection so terrifying they frighten even the most stalwart among us.

"Simple Simon?" Please. We know why Simon is simple. He's lost his humanity and turned into a flesh-eating, brain-consuming ghoul.

Did you ever wonder why Little Bo Peep was never without her shepherd's crook? Without a doubt it was developed in the Middle Ages as a defensive weapon against a Zombie invasion. A properly wielded crook can dispatch both the human and animal undead. And there is perhaps no more vicious creature than a Zombie sheep.

Jack Sprat? Zombie.

The Queen of Hearts? Hello? She cut out hearts of knaves. Definitely zombie.

The aforementioned Humpty Dumpty? The word is he tasted like chicken.

While it would be easy for you, dear reader, to cast this book aside as another parody or attempt to gain a few cheap laughs. I beg you, do not fall into this trap. Dig deeper and accept this tome for the serious piece of Zombie scholarship it is. For in learning how our ancestors confronted and conquered their own Zombie apocalypses we modern humans may find the strength and methods to do the same.

Read on and learn. And in the meantime keep a sharp eye and an even sharper machete ready to confront the coming Zombie menace.

And if you see a feverish owl or pussycat coming your way or worst of all, a Zombie sheep?

Run!

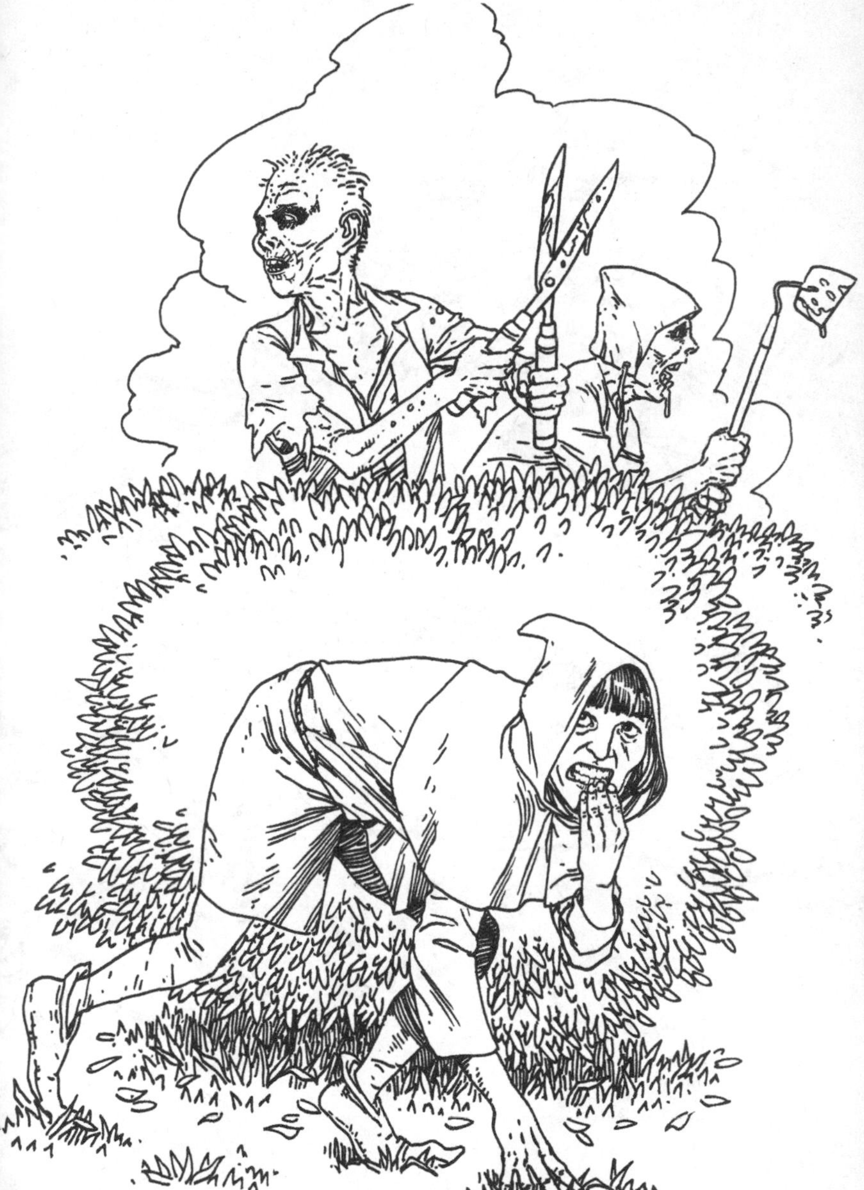

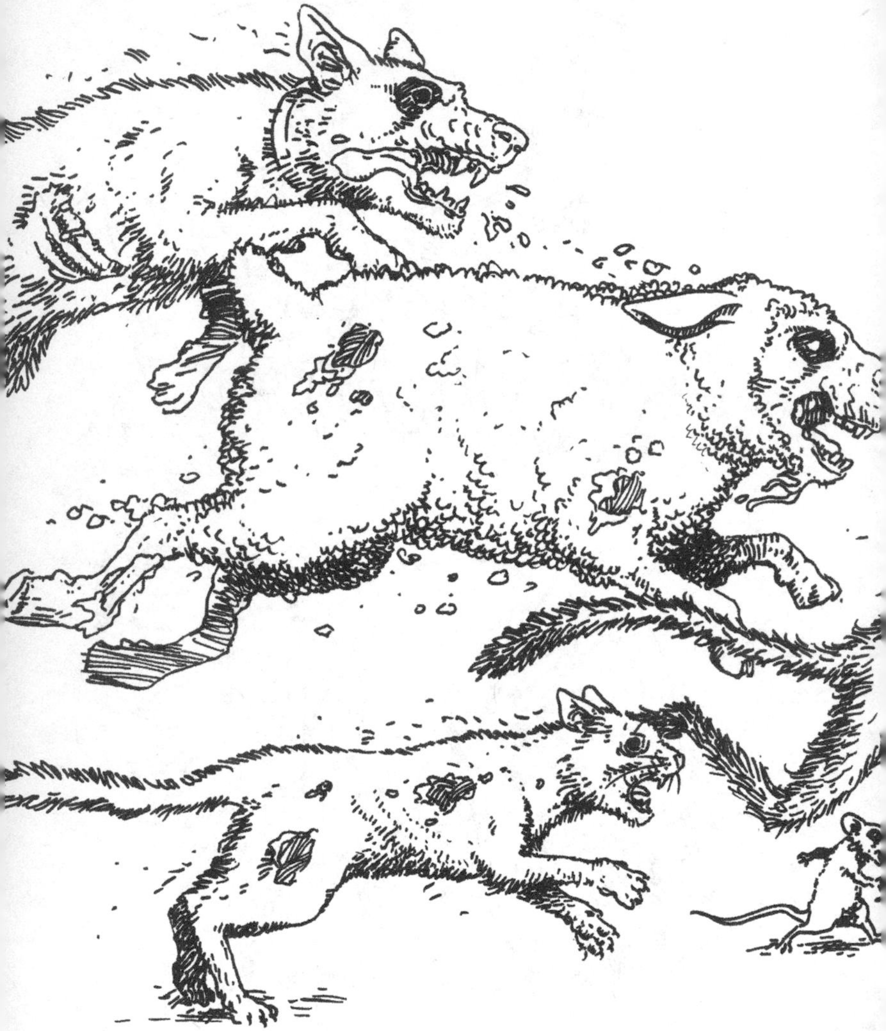

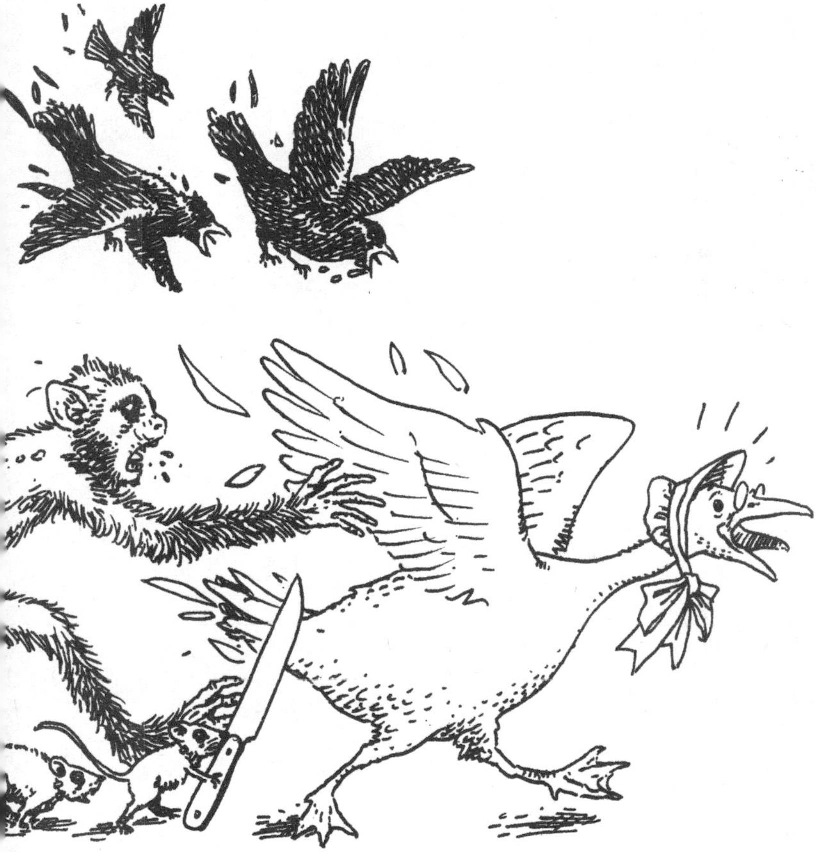

JACK
AND
JILL

Went Up to Kill

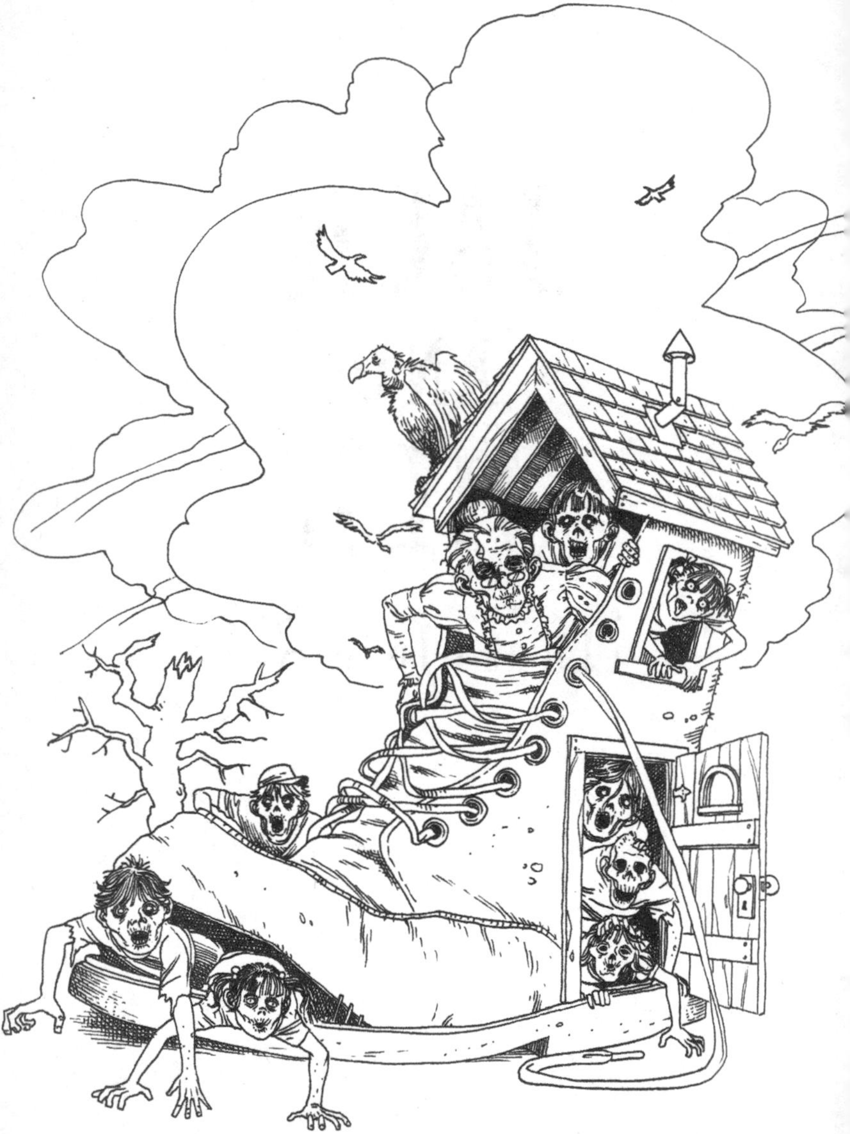

There Was an Old Zombie Woman Who Lived in a Shoe

There was an old Zombie woman who lived in a shoe.
  She ate so many children, she was covered in goo;
She gave them a chomp and tore open their heads;
Then they all turned and became the Undead.

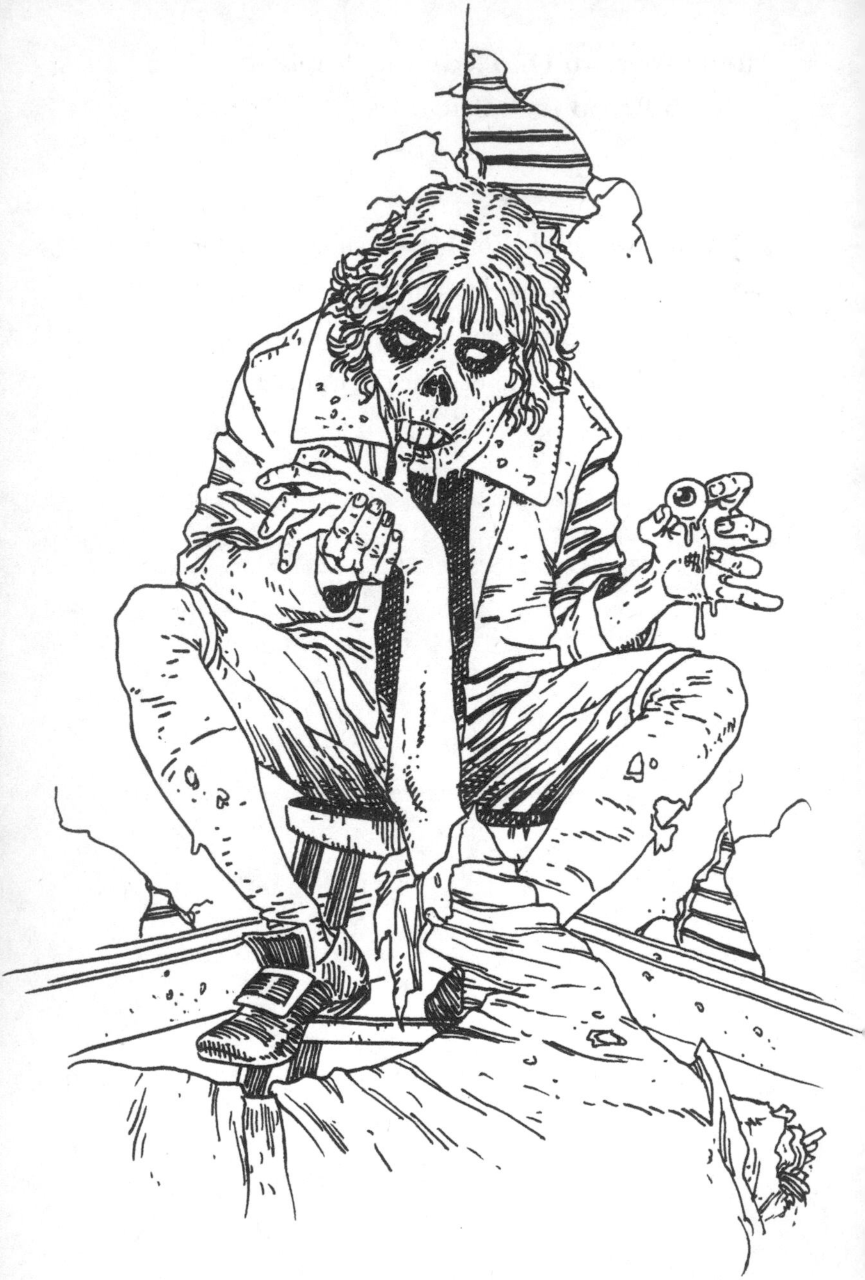

Little Jack Horner
   Sat in the corner,
Eating somebody's eye;
He chowed down on a thumb,
It had come from a bum,
And said, "What a good Zombie am I!"

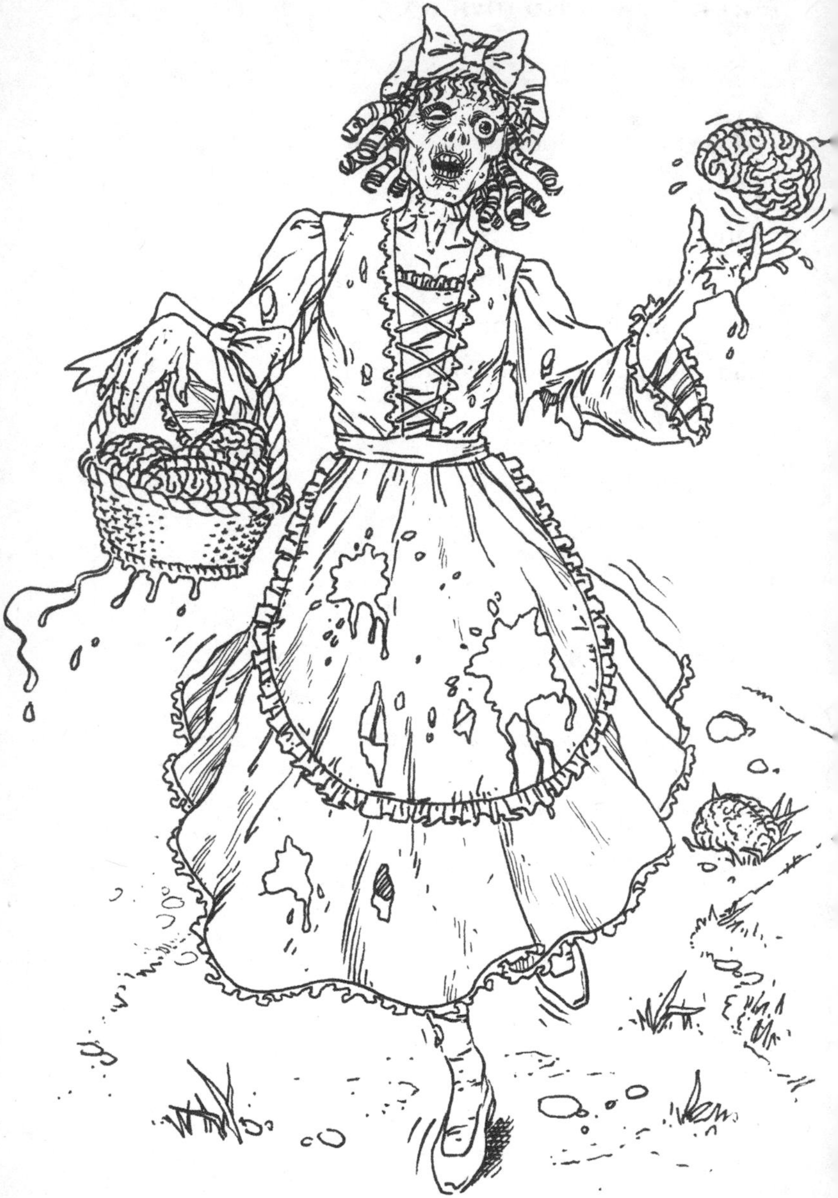

A-tisket, a-tasket
A green and yellow basket
I stole the brains o' my love
And on the way I dropped it,
I dropped it,
I dropped it,
And on the way I dropped it.
A little Zombie boy picked them up and put them in his
pocket.

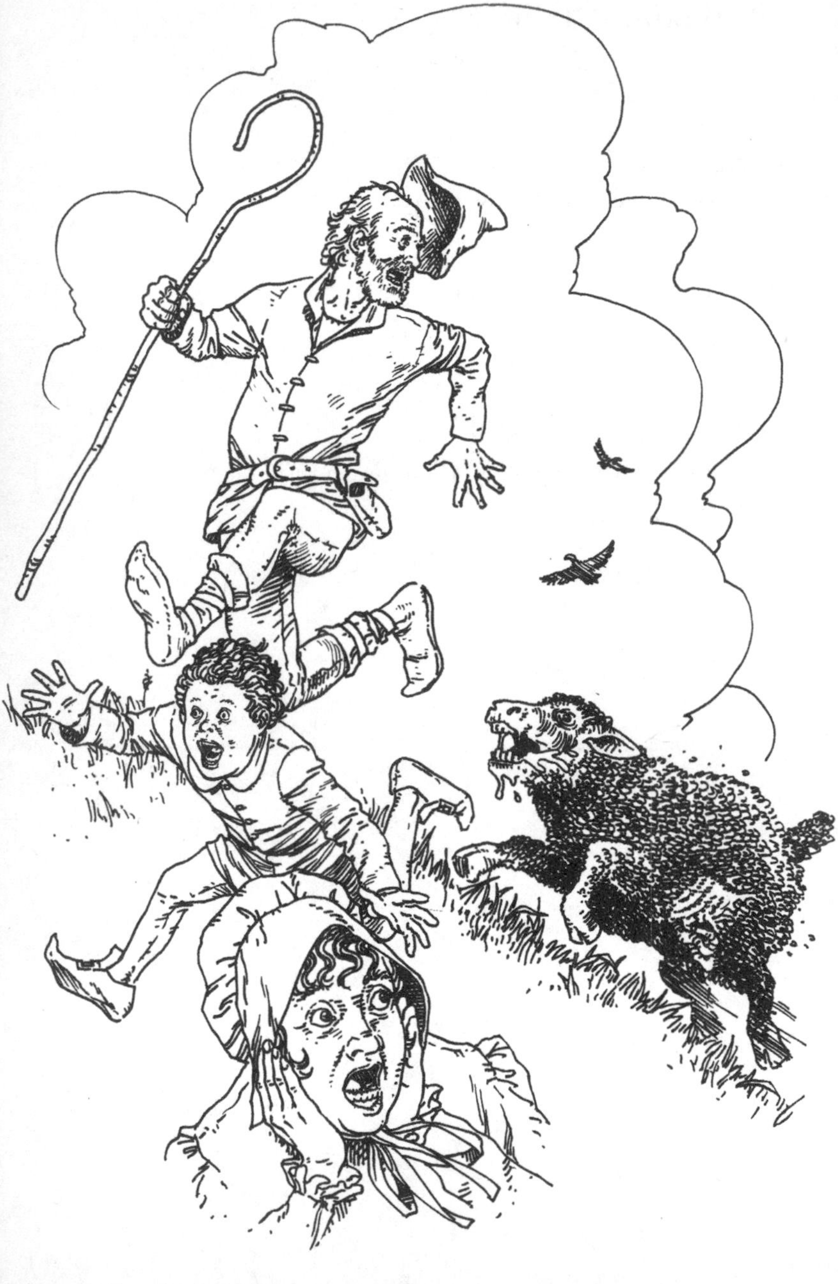

Baa, baa, Zombie sheep,
Have you eaten flesh?
Yes sir, yes sir,
It was nice and fresh.
We just ate the master,
Already ate the dame,
Let's go eat the little boy
Who lives down the lane.

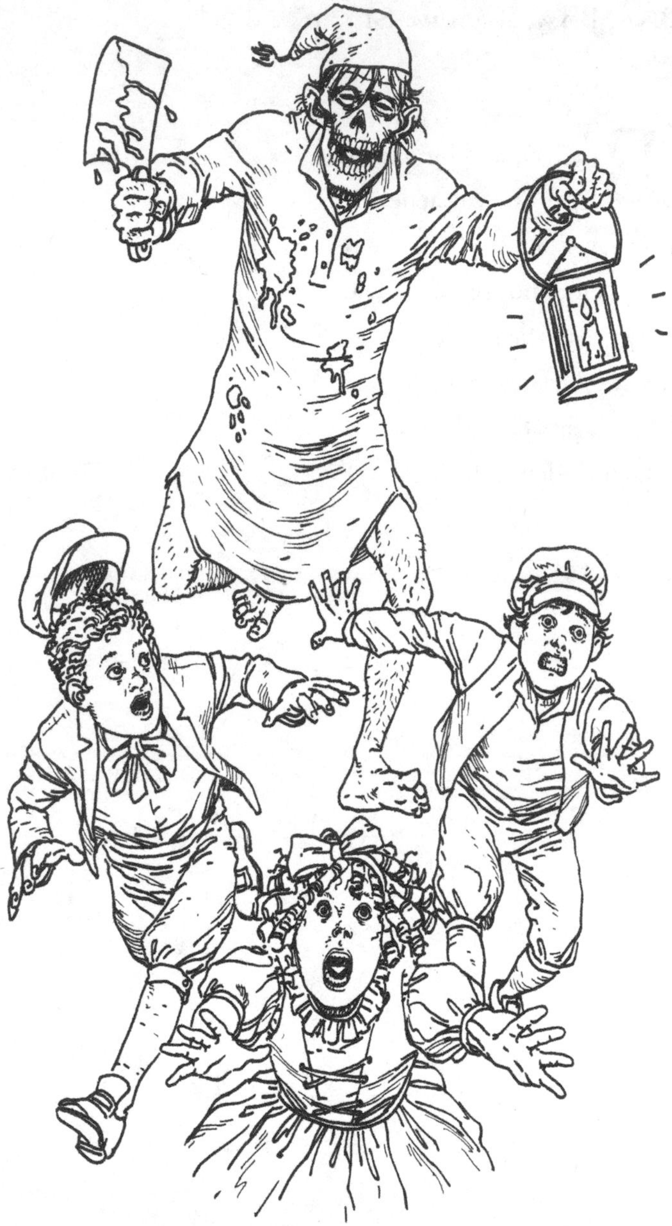

Zombie Willie Winkie runs through the town,
Upstairs and downstairs brains chowing down,
Tapping at the window and scratching at the lock,
Are all the children in their beds?
Is the shotgun cocked?

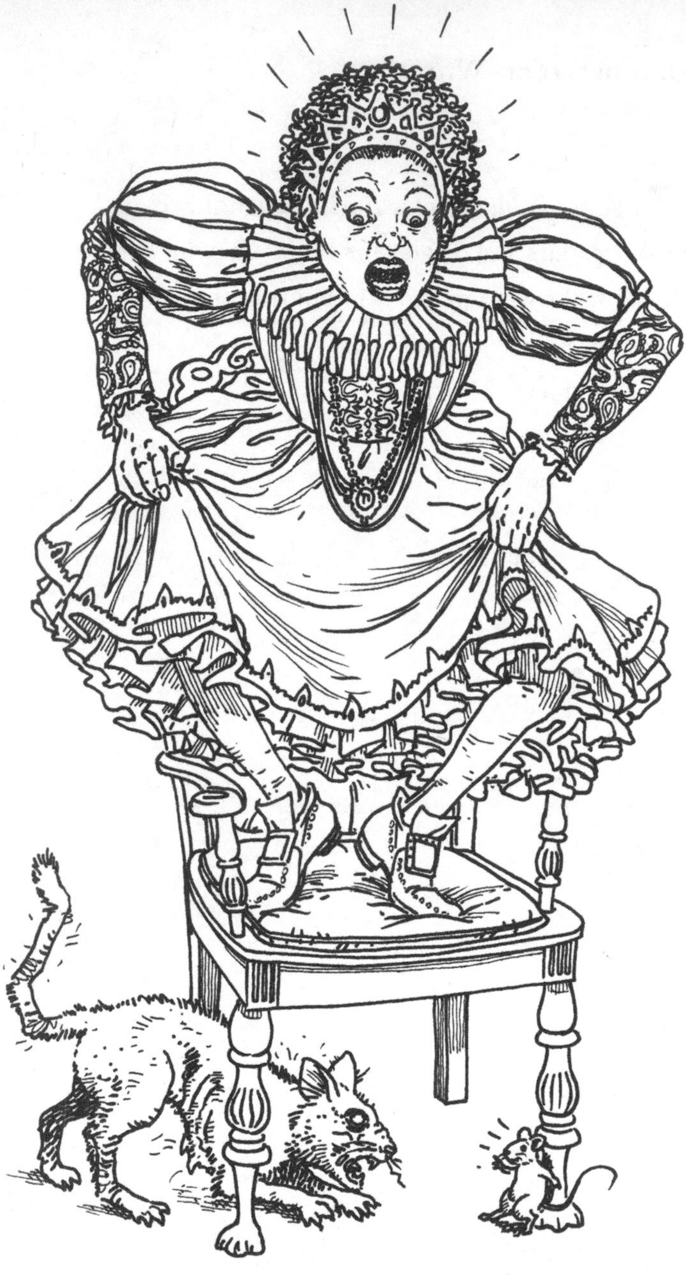

Zombiecat, zombiecat, where have you been?
I've been up to London to devour the Queen.
Zombiecat, zombiecat, what did you dare?
I want to eat the little mouse under the chair.
MEOWW!

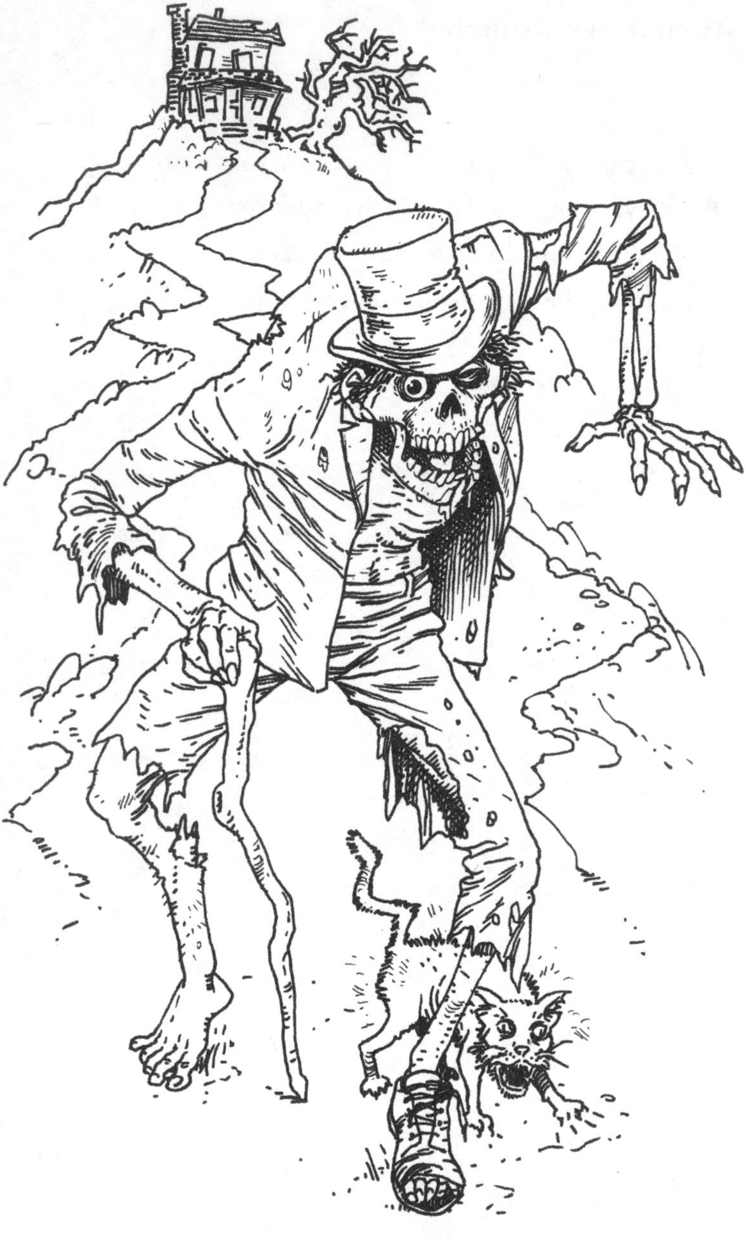

There was an Undead man, and he walked an Undead mile.
He found some flesh and brains upon a crooked stile.
He ate a crooked cat, then he ate a crooked mouse.
And they were all undead together in a little revenant house.

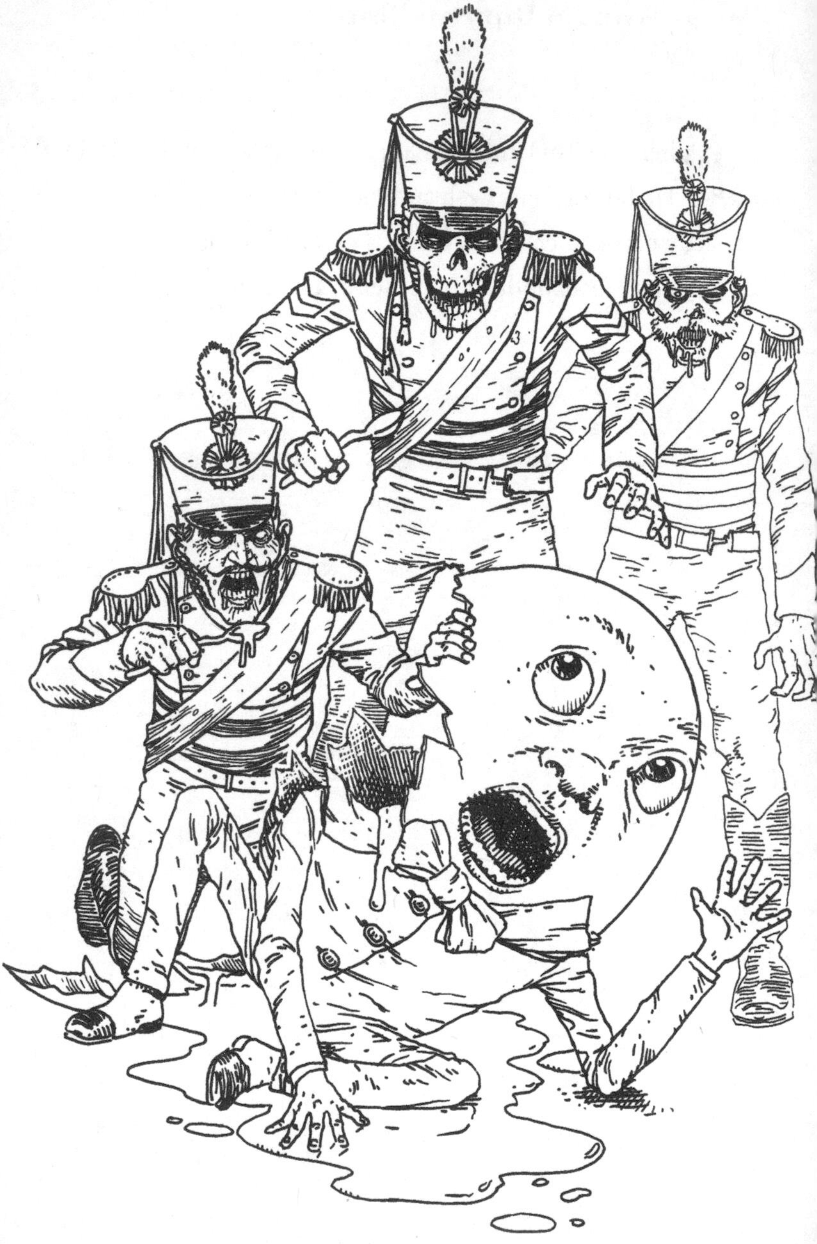

Humpty Dumpty

Humpty Dumpty sat on a wall,
Humpty Dumpty had a great fall.
All the king's Zombie horses and the king's Zombie men
Thought Humpty Dumpty tasted like chicken.

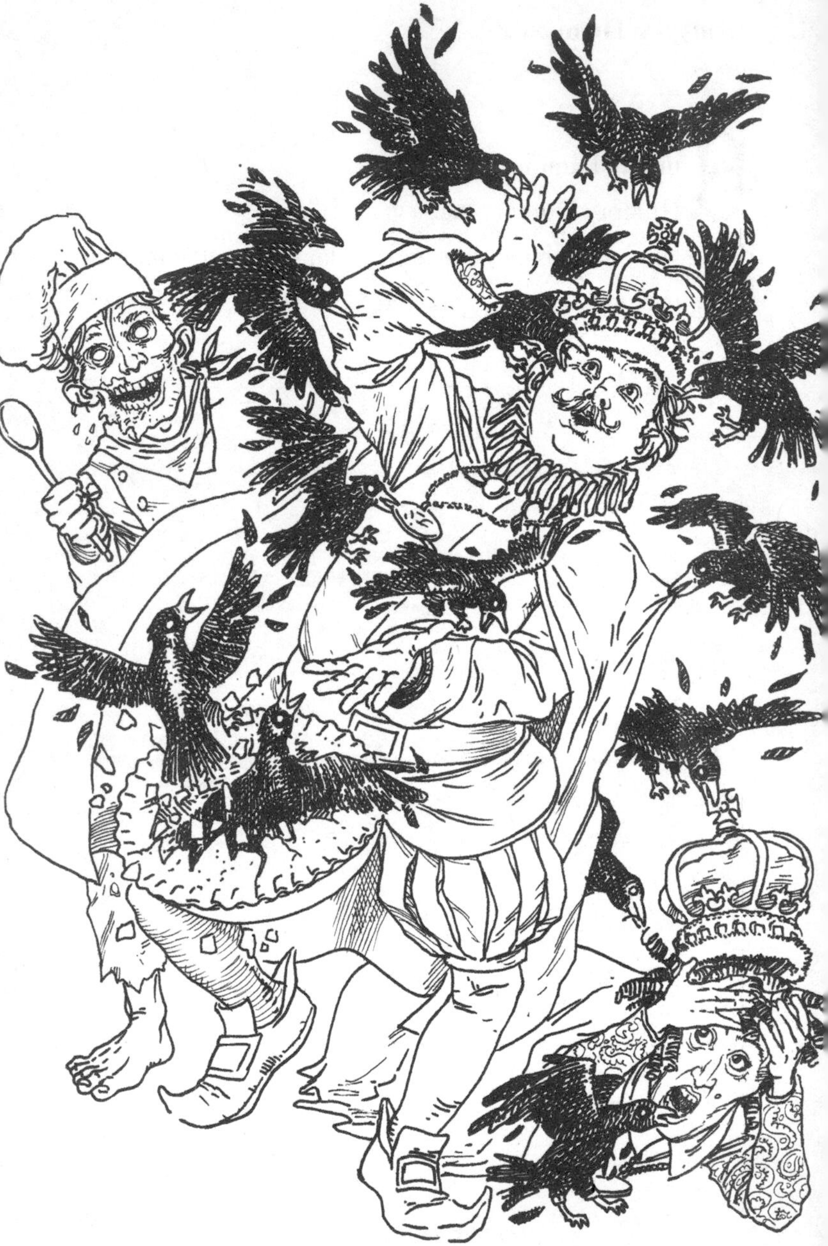

Sing a song of sixpence,
A pocket full of eyes.
Four and twenty blackbirds,
Baked in a pie.

When the pie was opened,
The birds began to sing;
Wasn't that an Undead dish?
To set before the king?

The king was in his counting house,
Sharpening his machete;
The queen was in the parlor,
Her brains were nice and runny.

The maid was in the garden,
Hanging out the clothes;
When down came a Zombie blackbird
And pecked off her nose.

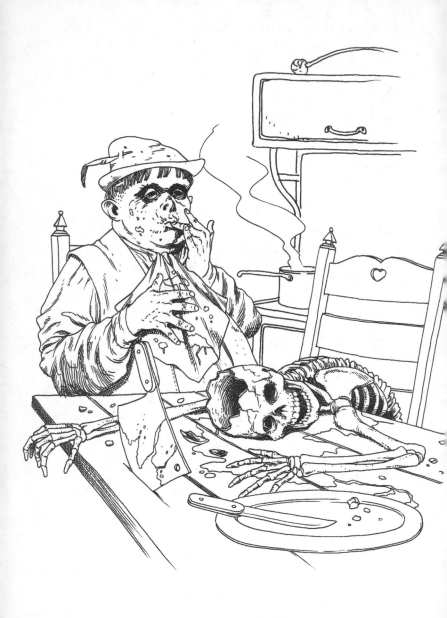

Jack Sprat Was a Revenant

Jack Sprat was a revenant.
He ate his poor wife's spleen.
He spread out her guts, munched her face,
Then licked the platter clean.

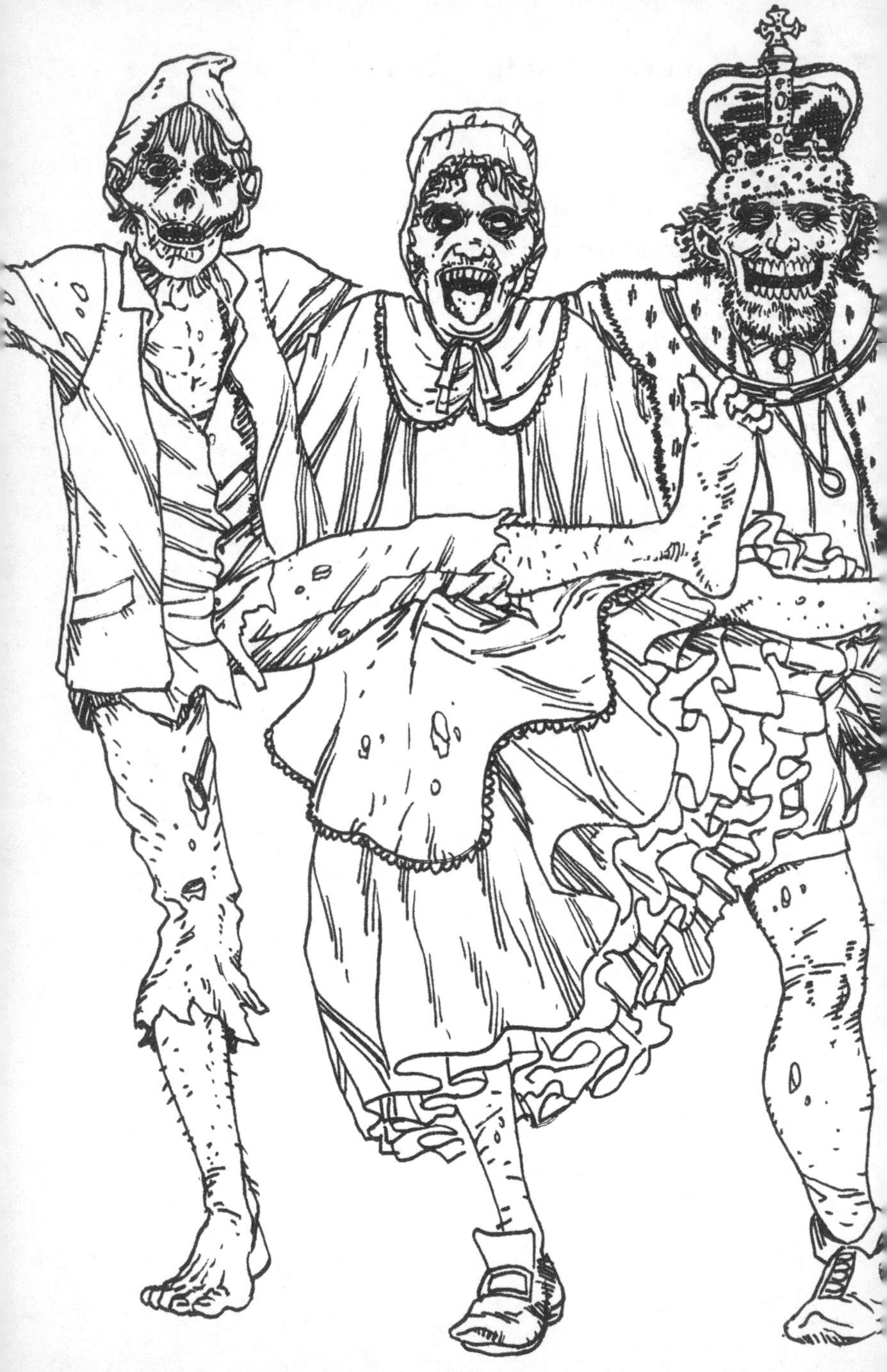

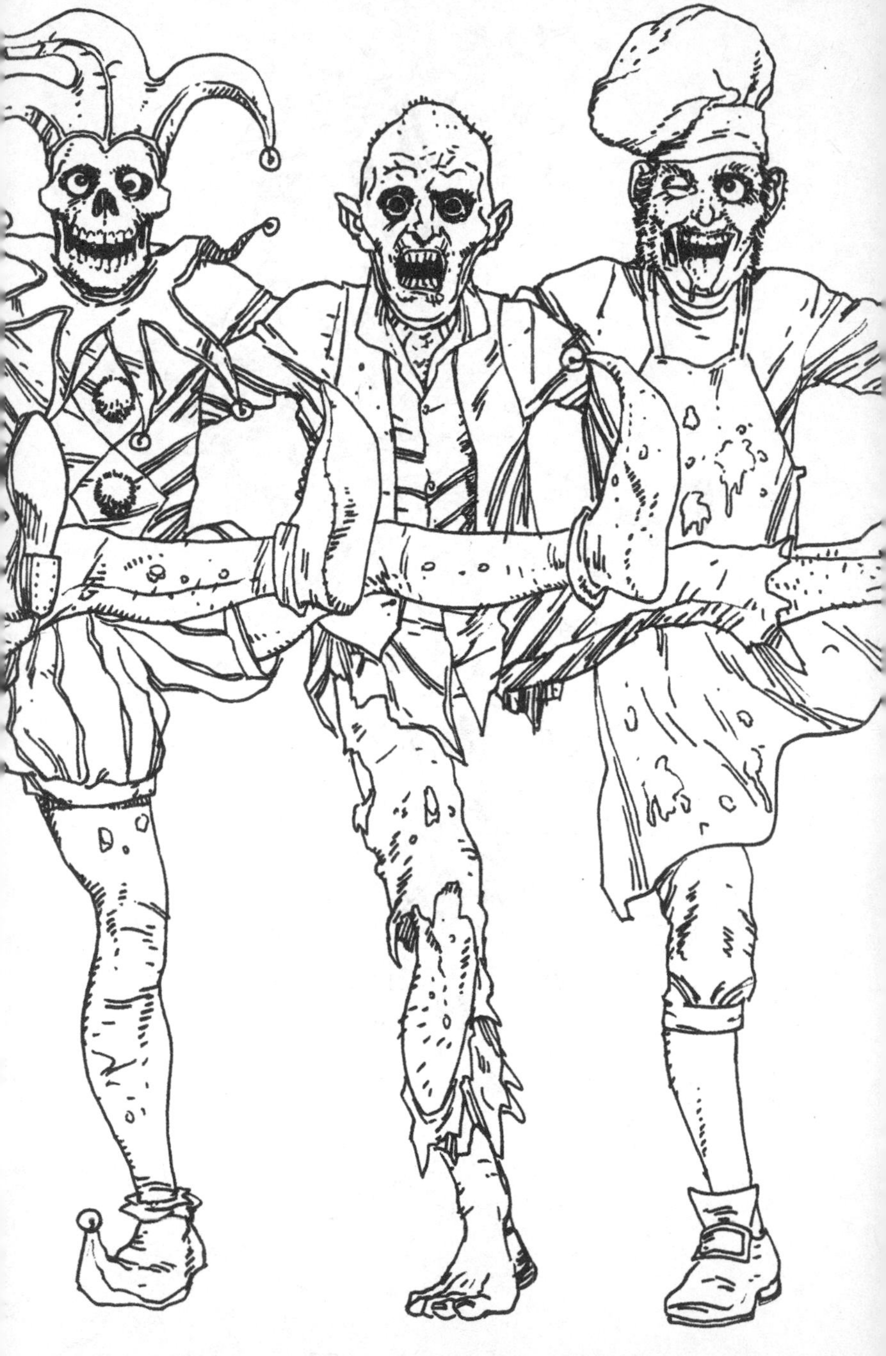

Jack and Jill Went Up to Kill

Jack and Jill went up to kill
They'd caught the Zombie virus.
Jack fell down and broke his crown,
And looked like Miley Cyrus.

Mary Jane was in the lane
Holding a machete.
She called for Nell to ring the bell
'Cause Jack and Jill were Zombies.

Then up Jack got and home did trot
As fast as he could shuffle;
To Old Dame Dob who proved tasty
Her screams they were not muffled.

Jill came in and she did grin
It scared us just to see her;
Mother vexed did cut off her head
To stop Zombie invaders.

Now Jack didn't care that Jill was dead
For Zombies cannot tell;
Then the townsfolk cut him down like her
And sent his undead ass to hell.

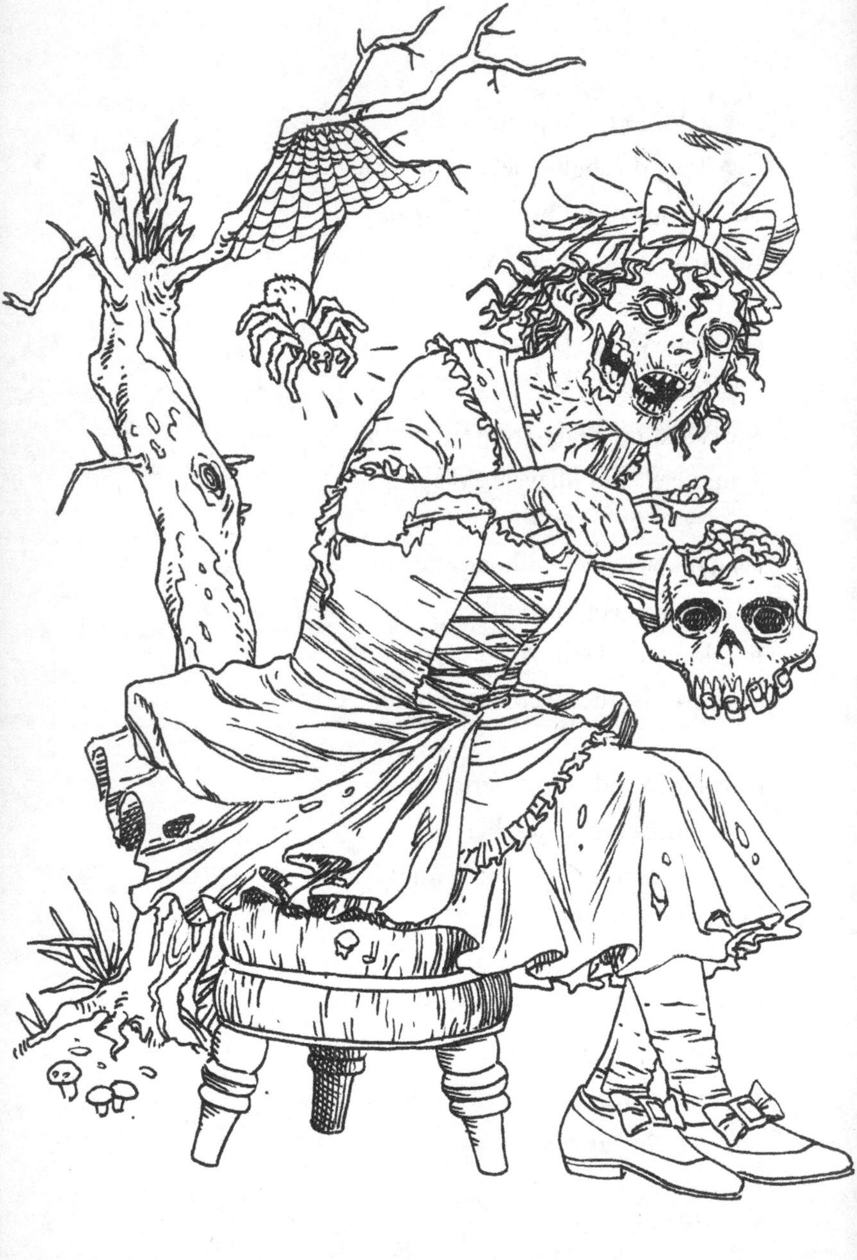

Little Miss Muffet Turned on a Tuffet

Little Miss Muffet turned on a tuffet,
Eating fresh brains all day;
Along came a human,
She added some cumin,
And munched the poor man away.

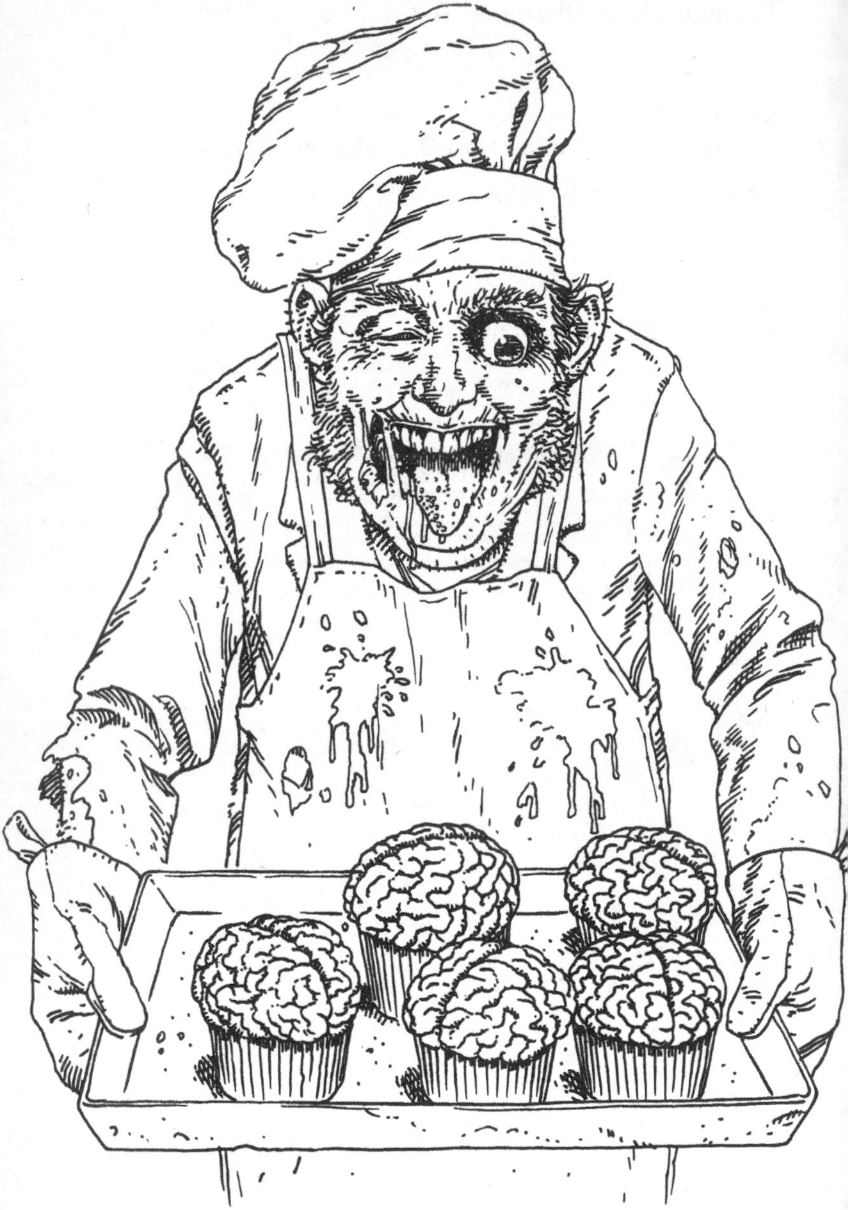

Do You Know the Undead Man?

Do you know the Undead man,
    With no right arm, and no left hand?
Do you know the Undead man,
Who lives right next door?

Yes, I know the Undead man,
I shot him twice and it was nice,
Now he's a really dead Undead man,
So please clean up the gore.

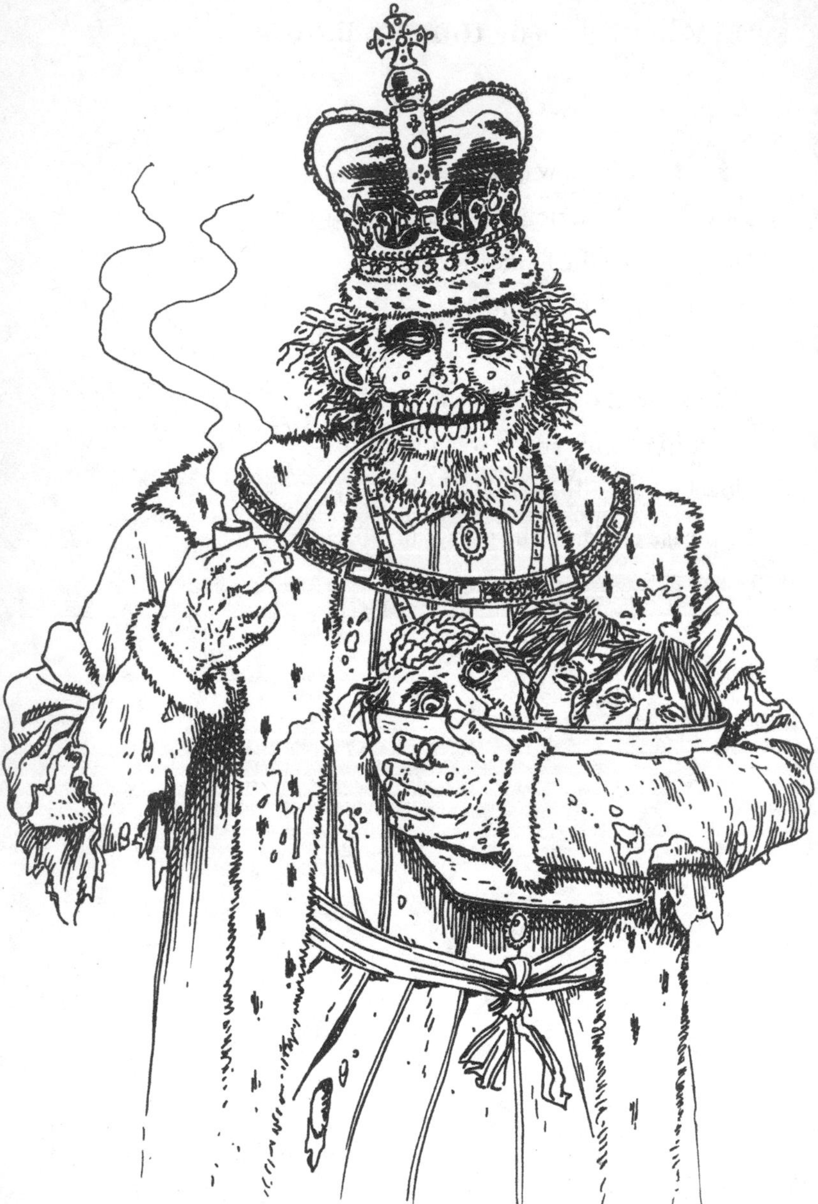

Old King Cole Is a Merry Old Ghoul

Old King Cole is a merry old ghoul,
And a new Zombie was he;
I hit him with a pipe, and stabbed him in his jowl
As he munched on his fiddlers three.
Every fiddler came back to life,
To very fine Zombies be;
So I turned and I ran, I can kill them again,
As Old King Cole ate his fiddlers three.

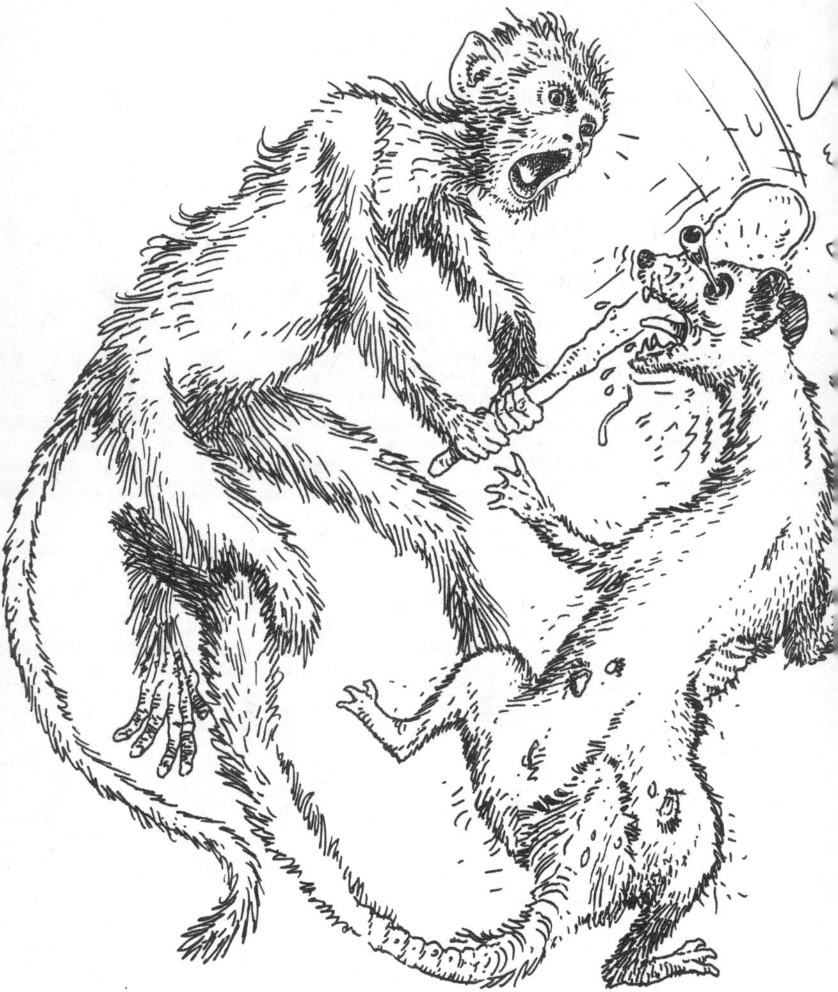

The Monkey and the Weasel

All around the cobbler's bench,
The monkey chased the weasel.
The monkey thought the brains were good,
Pop! goes the weasel.

The monkey now he is Undead,
And looking for a free meal—
That's the way the Zombie goes,
Pop! goes the weasel.

Jimmy's not got whooping cough
And Timmy has no measles
That's the way the virus grows
Pop! goes the weasel.

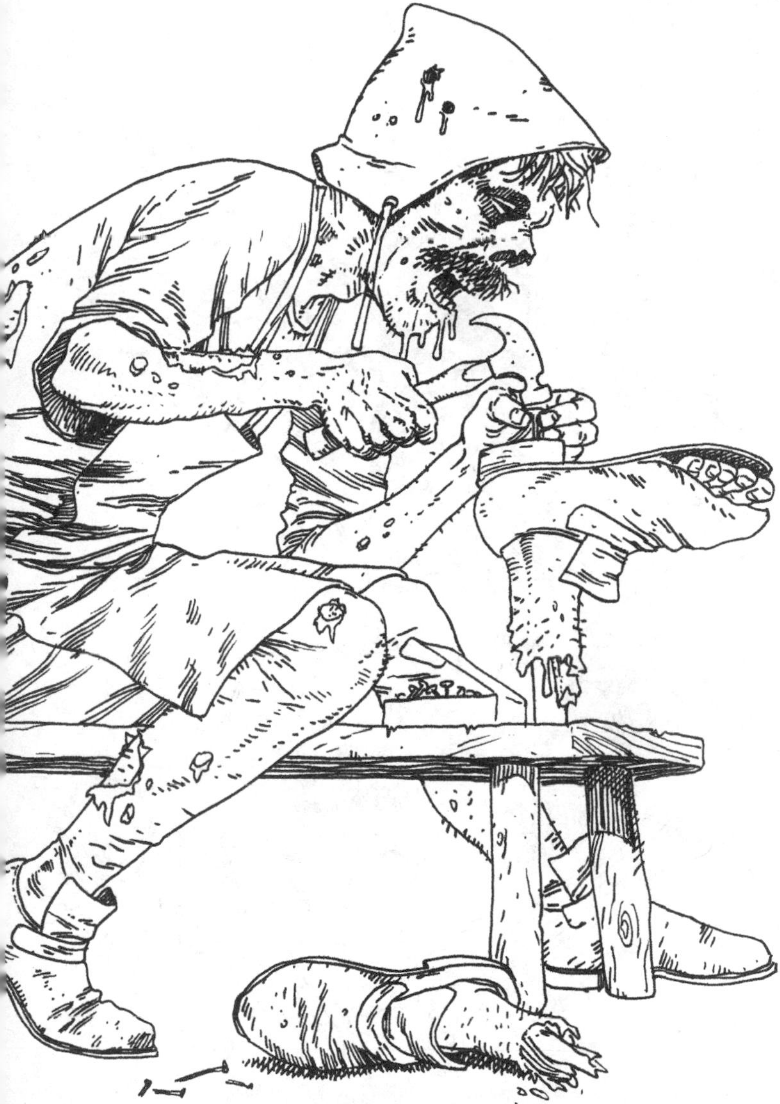

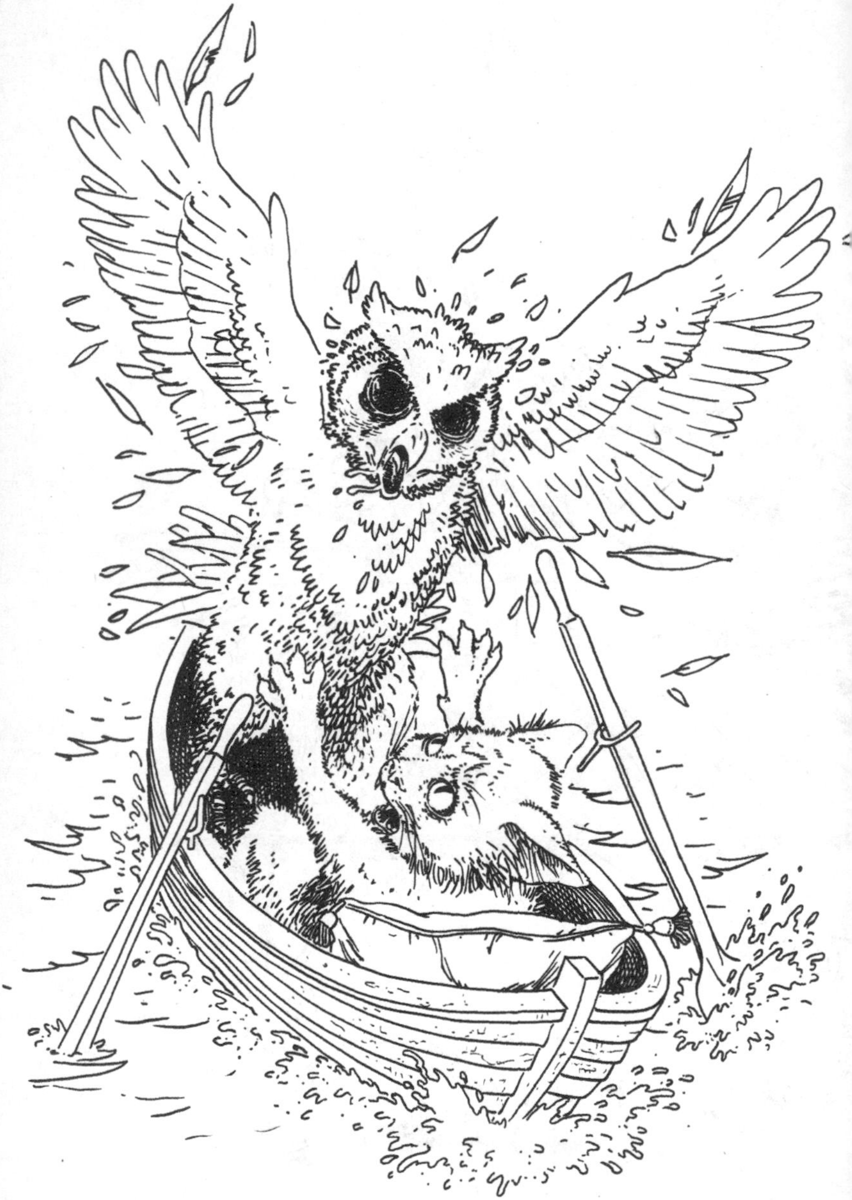

The Owl and the Pussycat

The Owl and the Pussycat went to sea
Because Zombies do not float:
They took a shotgun, and a "no Zombie doctrine"
In their beautiful pea green boat.

The Owl looked up to the stars above,
And sang to a small guitar,
"O pussycat, pussycat, my love,
We're away from the undead out here,
Don't turn,
Don't turn!
For I would hate to have to shoot you!"

Pussy said to the Owl, "You elegant fowl,
How charmingly sweet you sing!
Oh! Let us not turn; for one of us would burn:
Let's hope the virus stays away."
They sailed away, for a year and a day,
To the land no Zombie knows;
But there in a wood a Zombie pig stood,
With flesh hanging off his nose,
His nose,
His nose,
With brains at the end of his nose.

"Dear Pig, don't come near us; you'll certainly fear us.
I'll blast you clean up to the sky."
Then Pussycat noticed that Owl looked feverish
And cocked the shotgun with a sigh.
"I'm sorry, my friend, but this virus must end."
And sent Owl to the nest in the sky.

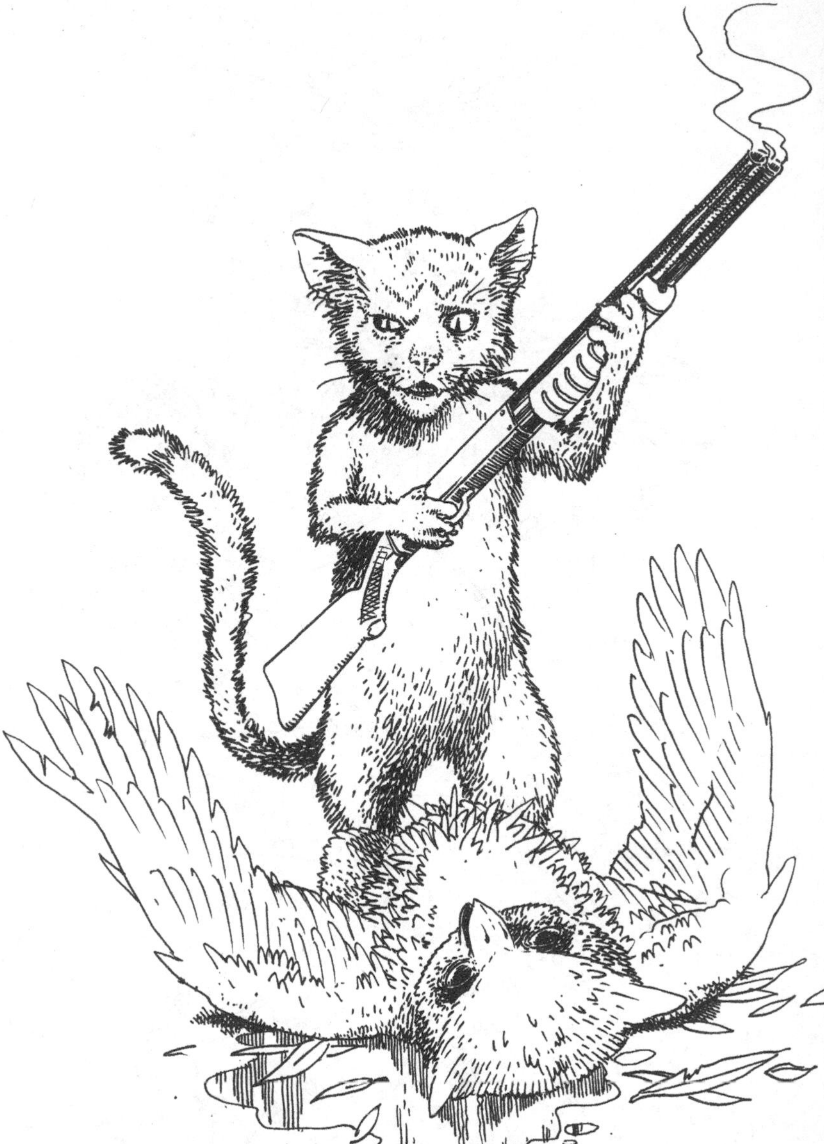

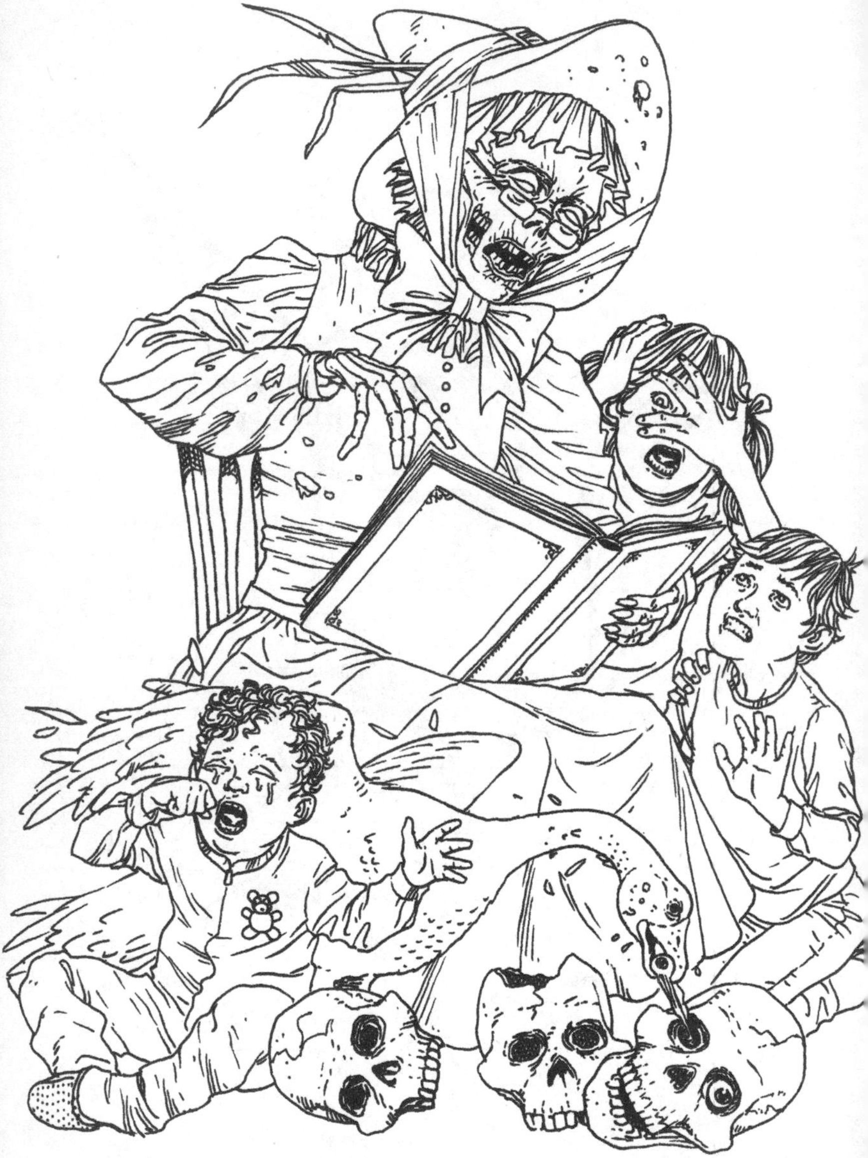

Brains! Brains! Mother Goose,
Or have you any femurs loose?
And I have thighs, my pretty fellow,
Half enough to fill a pillow.
Here are spleens, take one or two,
And lungs to make a bed for you.

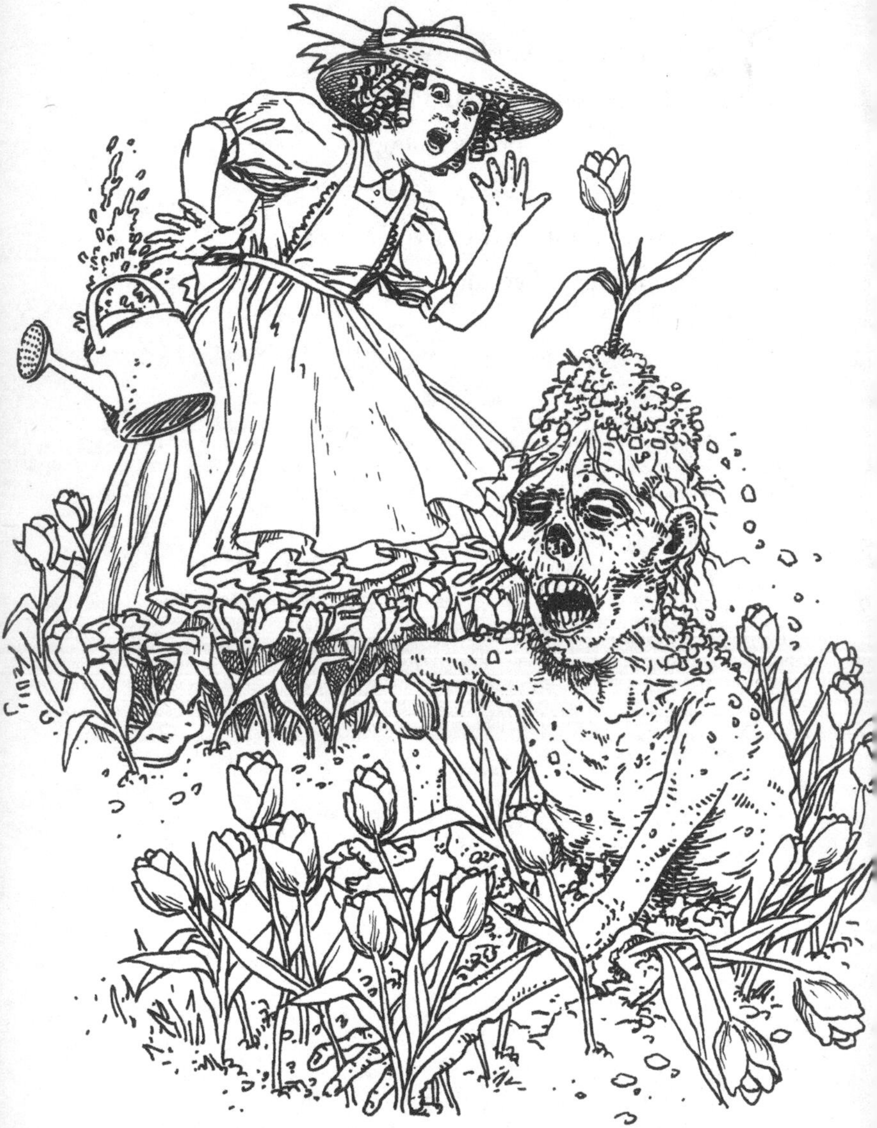

Mary, Mary, Quite Contrary

Mary, Mary, quite contrary,
How does your garden grow?
With Zombie yells and revenant spells,
And Undead maids all in a row.

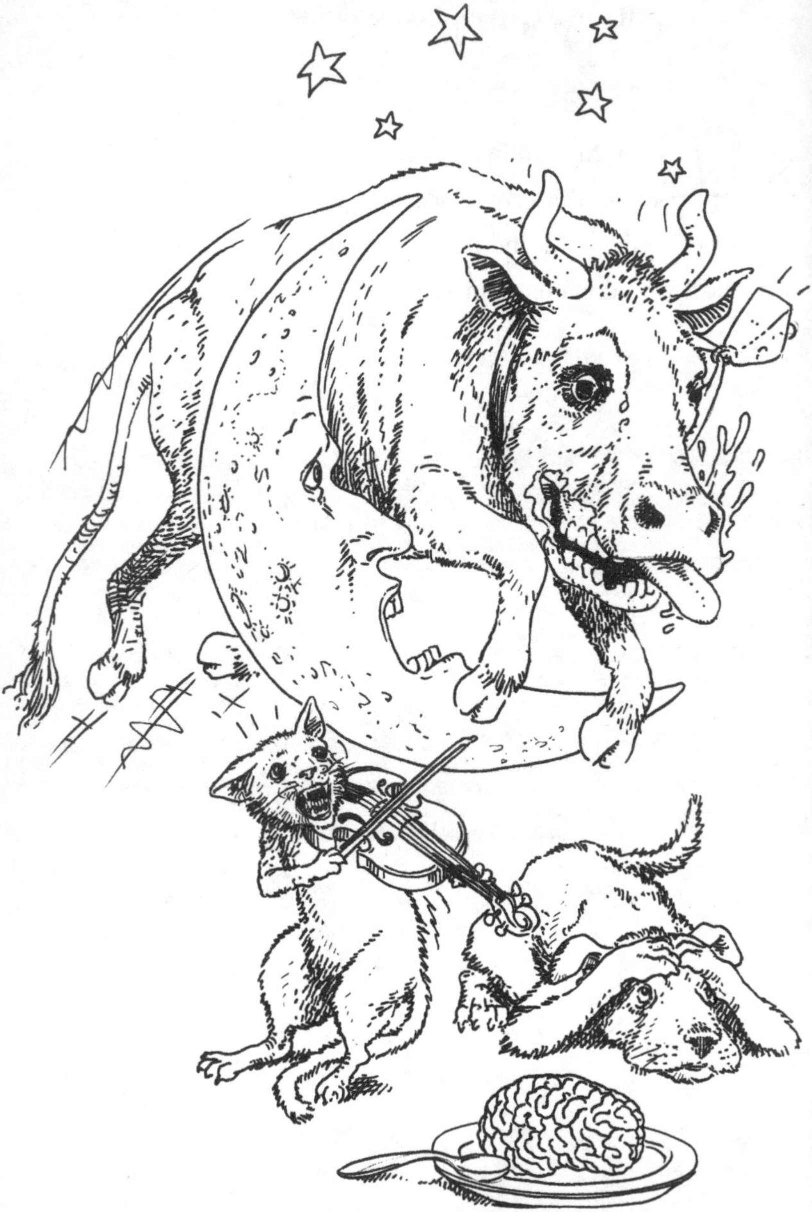

HEY! DIDDLE, DIDDLE!

Hey! Diddle, diddle,
The cat and the fiddle,
The cow turned under the moon;
The Zombie dog laughed to see such sport,
And ate their brains with a spoon.

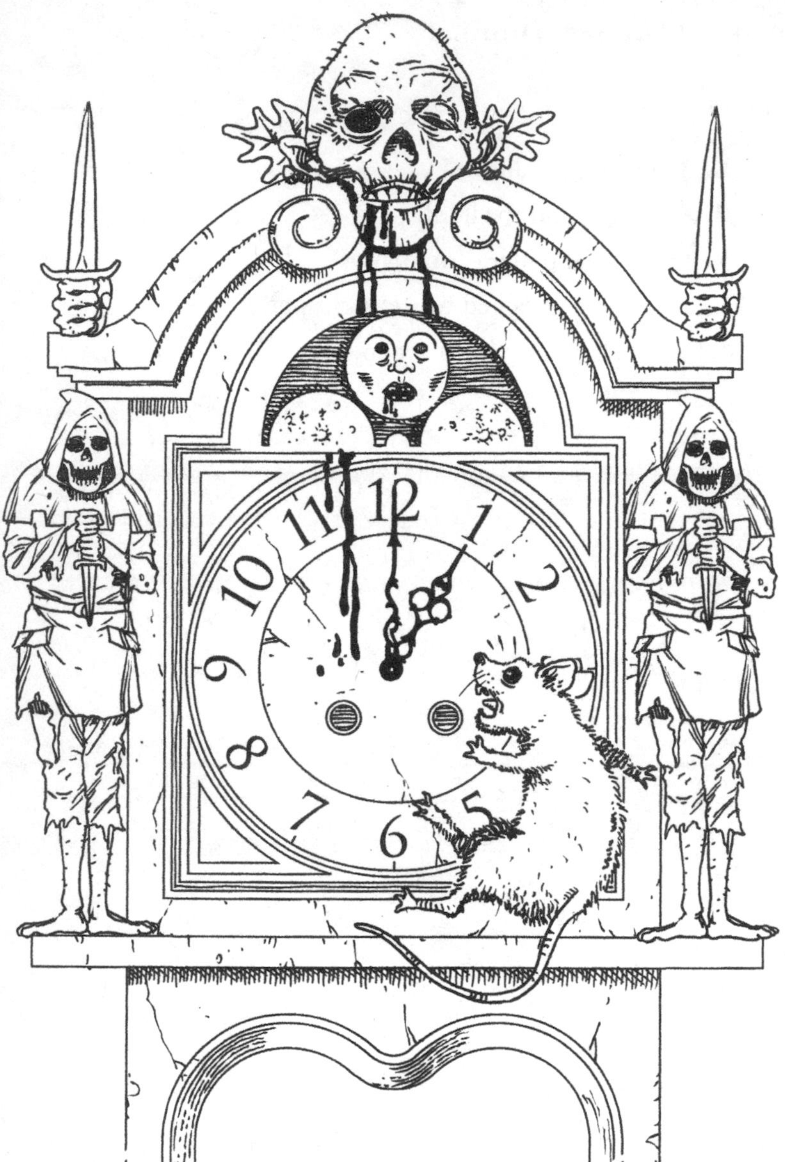

Hickory, Dickory, Dock!

Hickory, dickory, dock!
The mouse upon a Zombie clock.
The clock bit once,
The mouse was turned,
Hickory, dickory, dock.

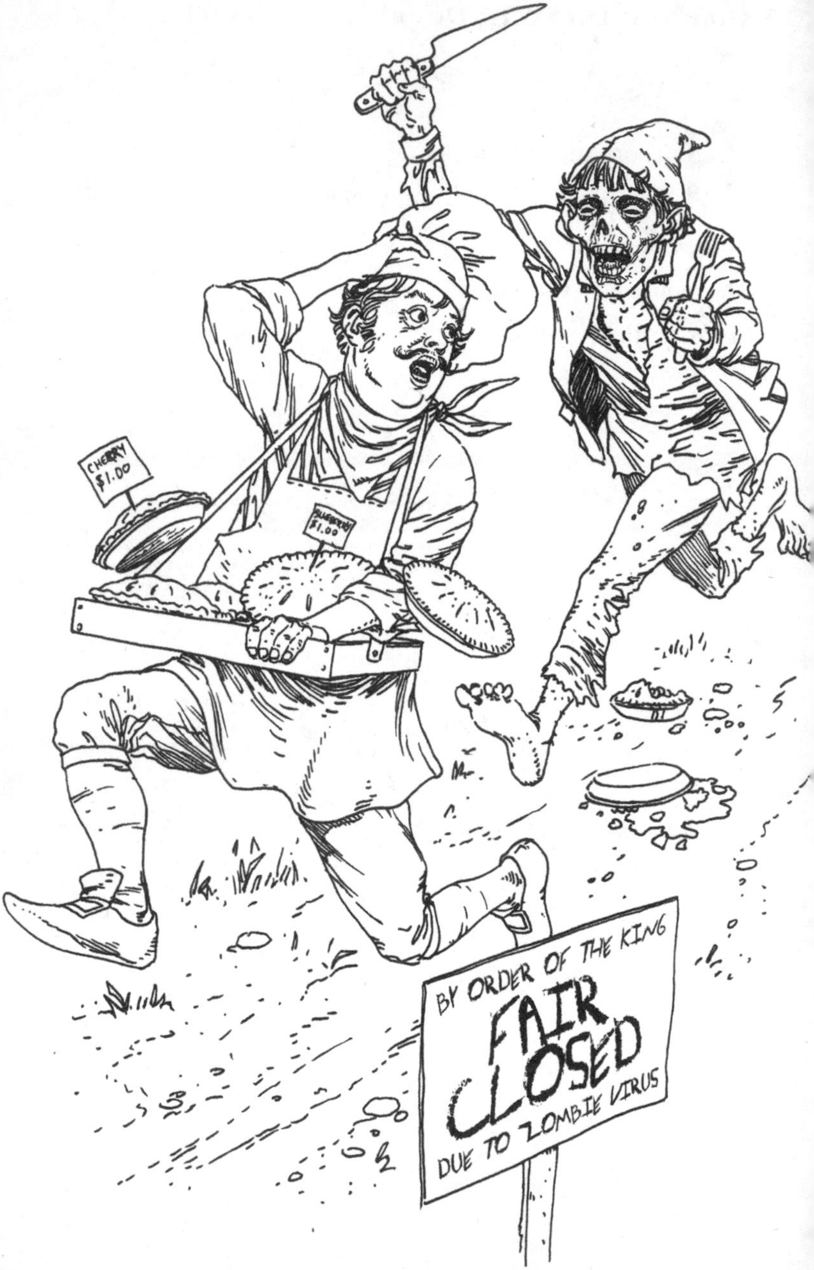
CHERRY
$1.00
$1.00
BY ORDER OF THE KING
FAIR
CLOSED
DUE TO ZOMBIE VIRUS

Zombie Simon

Zombie Simon ate the pie man,
  Going to the fair;
Said Zombie Simon to the pie man
"Let me taste your hair!"

Said the pie man to Zombie Simon,
"Show me first your penny."
So Zombie Simon chomped the pie man,
Who tasted good as any.

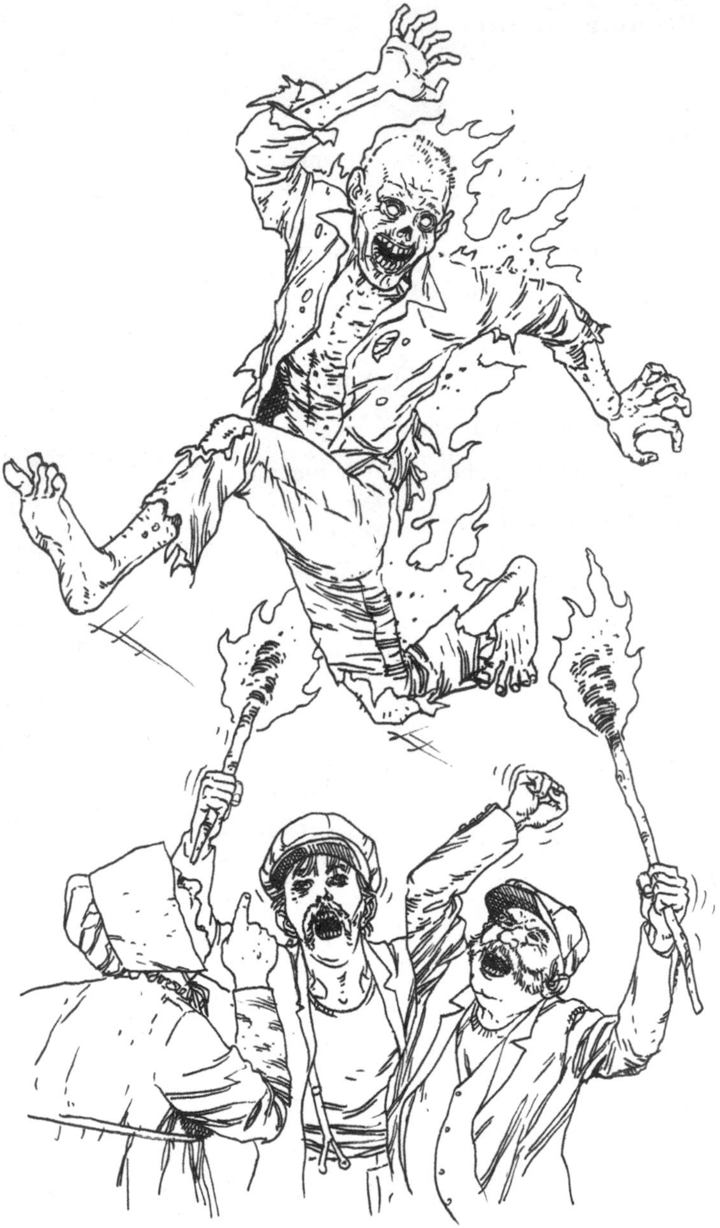

Jack be nimble,
Jack be quick,
Jack kills a Zombie
With a candlestick.

Jump so high
And do not tarry
Or Zombies away
You will carry.

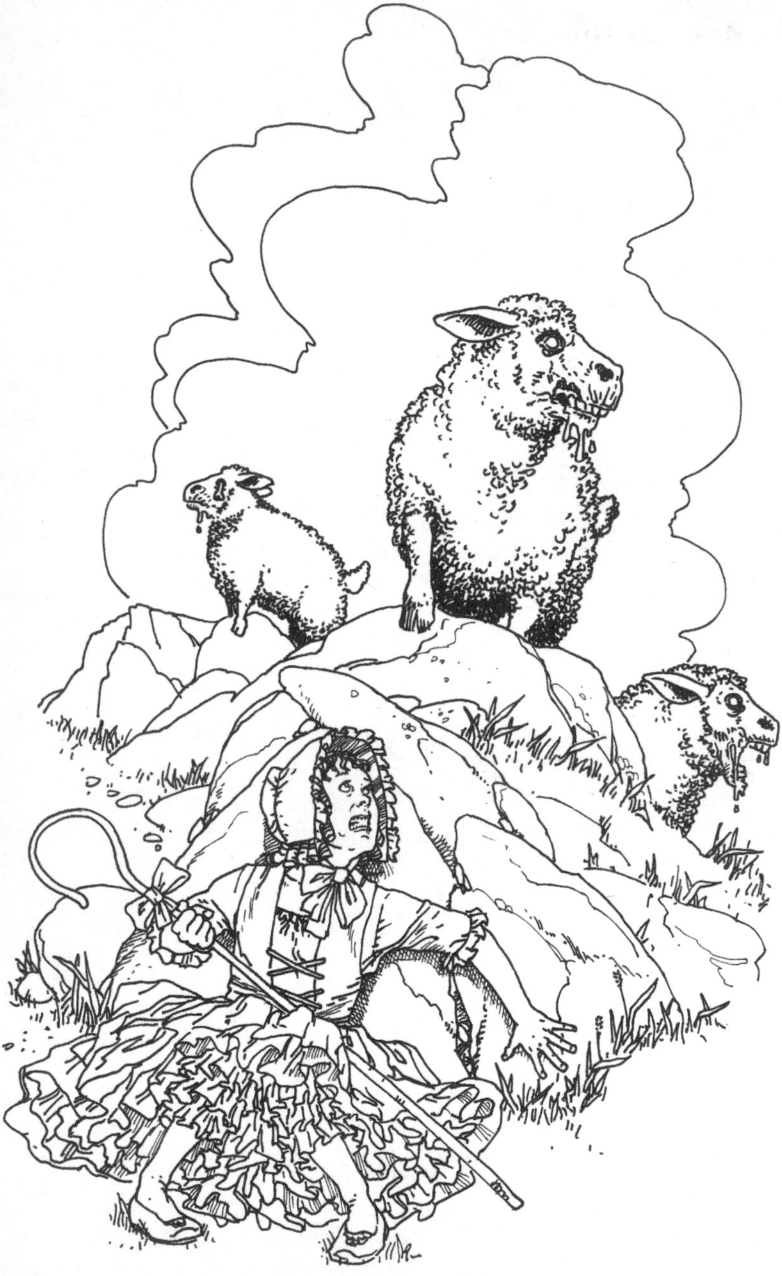

Little Bo Peep

Little Bo Peep has lost her sheep,
She doesn't know they've turned into Zombies;
Leave them alone or they'll come home,
Bringing entrails behind them.

Little Bo Peep fell fast asleep
And dreamt she heard them bleating,
But when she awoke found it was no joke,
For they were all flesh eating.

Then up she took her little crook
Determined to smash their brains in.
She found them indeed, but it made her heart bleed,
For they left dead folks behind them.

It happened one day, as Bo Peep did stray
Into a meadow hard by,
There she started to slide on their gooey insides
All hung on a tree to dry.

She heaved a sigh, and wiped her eye,
And over the hillocks went killing,
And tried what she could, as a shepherdess should,
To stop Zombie sheep from spreading.

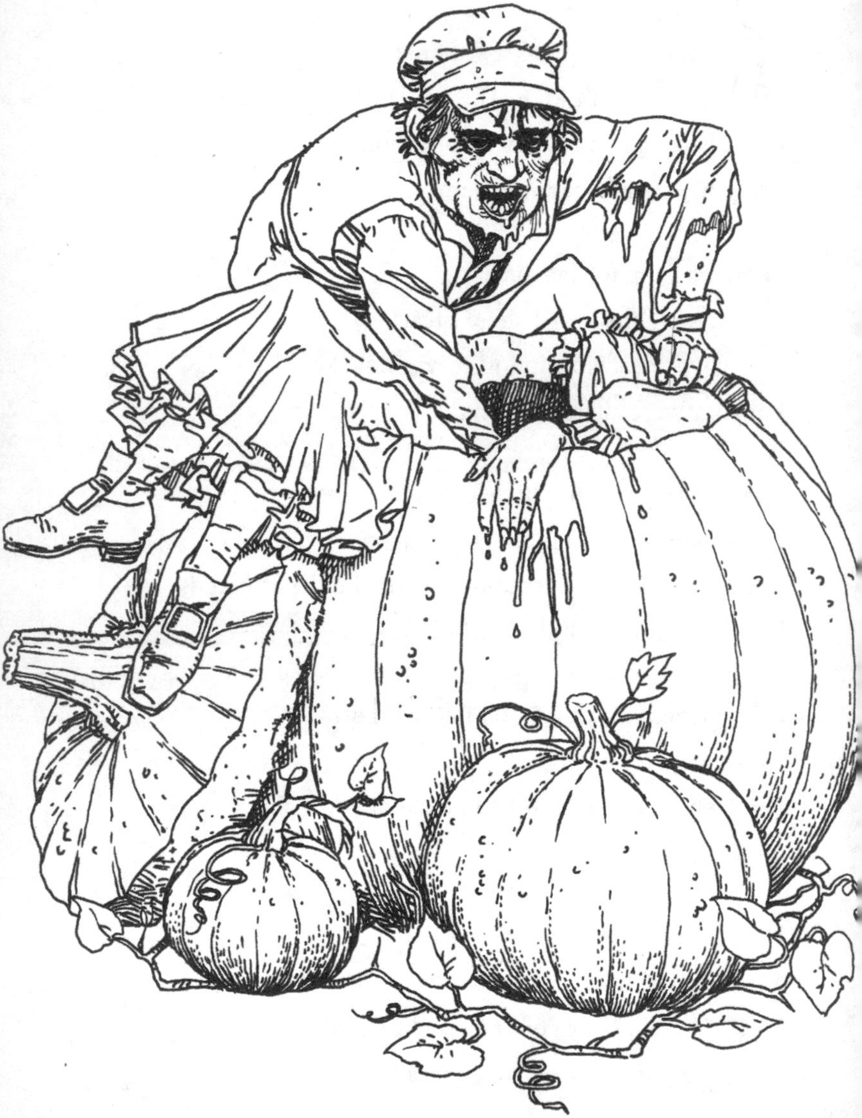

Peter, Peter, Fresh Brain Eater

Peter, Peter, fresh brain eater,
    Chomped his wife and she was sweeter!
He ate her brains before they smelled,
And thought she tasted pretty swell!

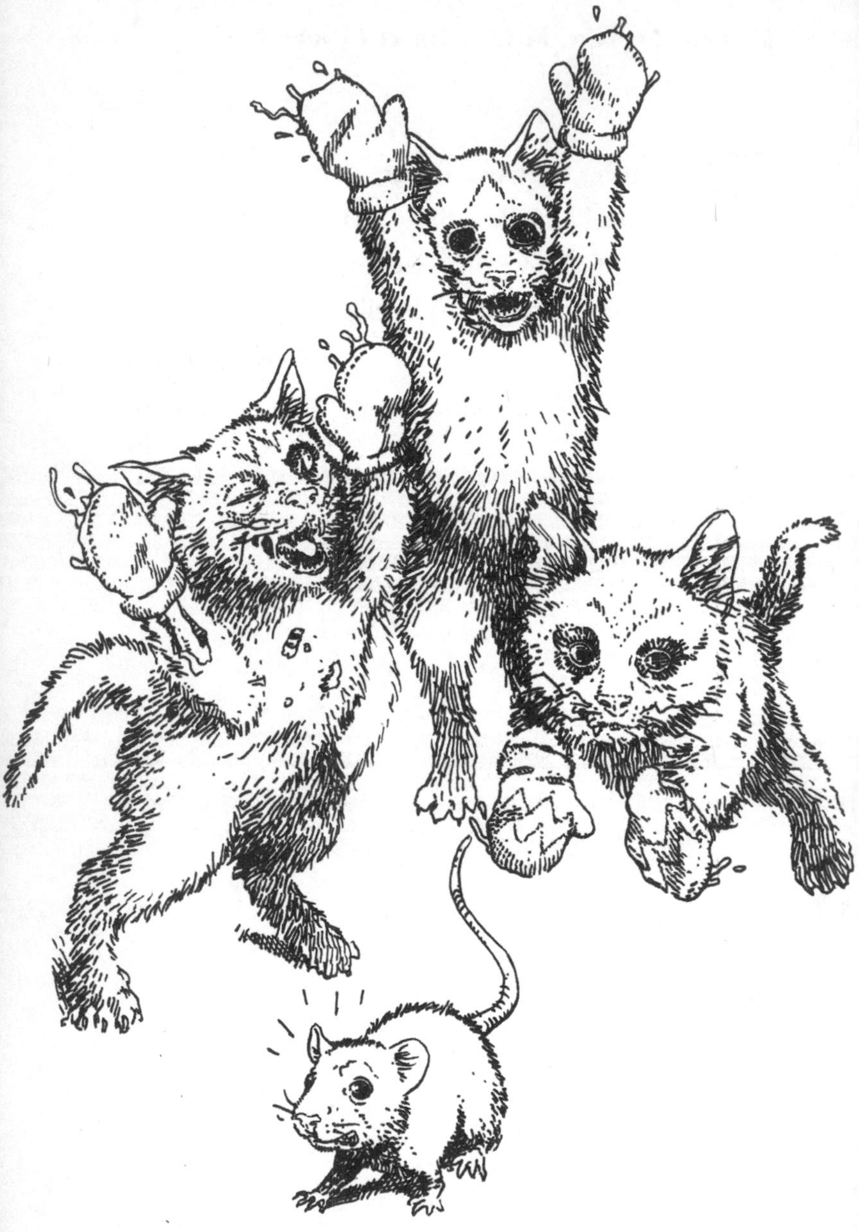

Three little kittens lost their mittens, as they began to turn,
"Oh Mother dear, we sadly fear that we have lost our
mittens."
"What! Lost your mittens, you naughty kittens!
Then you have no brain pie."
"Meeow, meeow, meeow, now we shall have no pie."

The three little kittens they found their mittens,
And they began to spew,
"Oh Mother dear, see here, see here
For we have found our mittens."
"Go away, go away, you zombie kittens
For you shall make me die."
"Meowbraiiins, meowbraiins . . . meowbraiins,
Now let us have brain pie."

The three little kittens put on their mittens
And soon ate up the mail guy,
"Oh Mother dear, we greatly fear
That we have soiled our mittens."
"What! Soiled your mittens, you naughty kittens!"
Then they began to cry, "Meeowbraaimnns, meeow, meeow."
Then they began to sigh.

The three little kittens they ate their mother

And soon began to cry,

"Oh Mother dear, you are not here

Your brain are upon our mittens."

"Brains! Brains! upon our mittens, we zombie kittens."

Do you smell a rat close by?

"Rat brains, rat brains, rat brains!" We smell a rat close by.

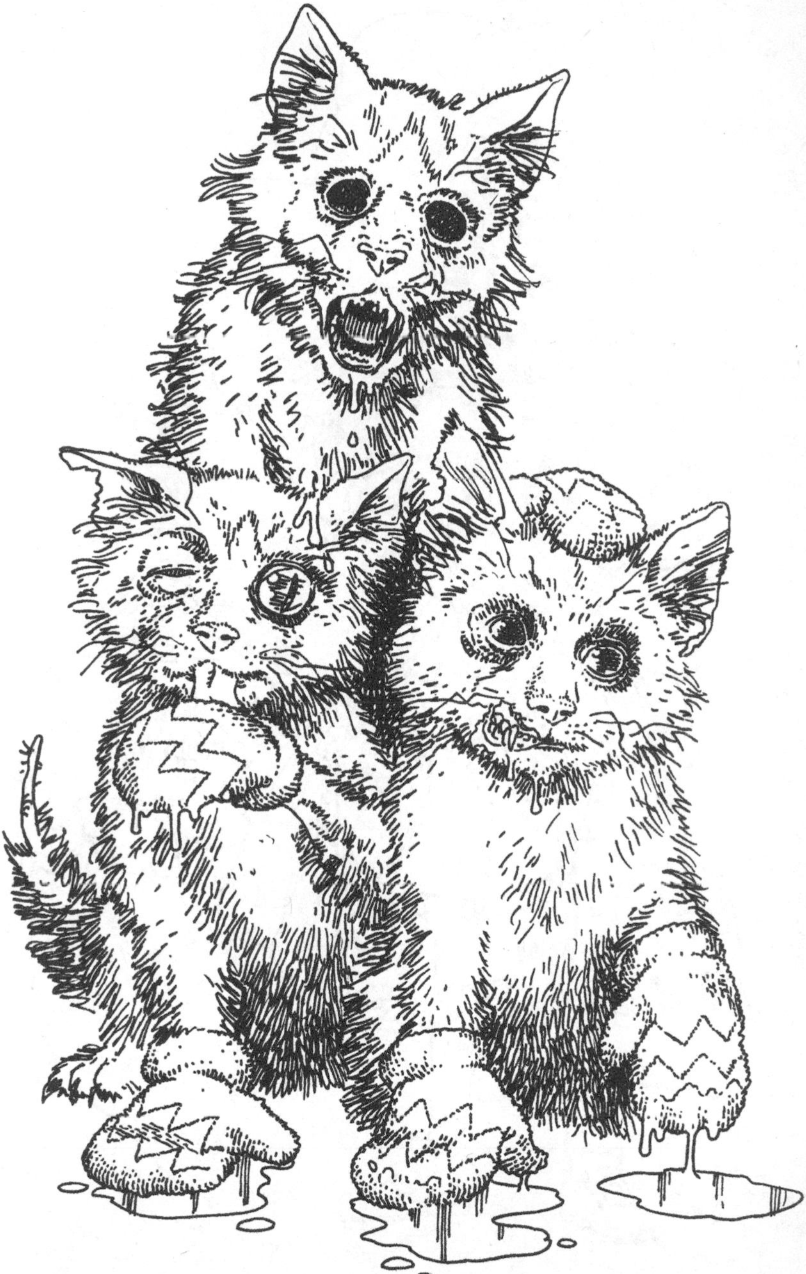

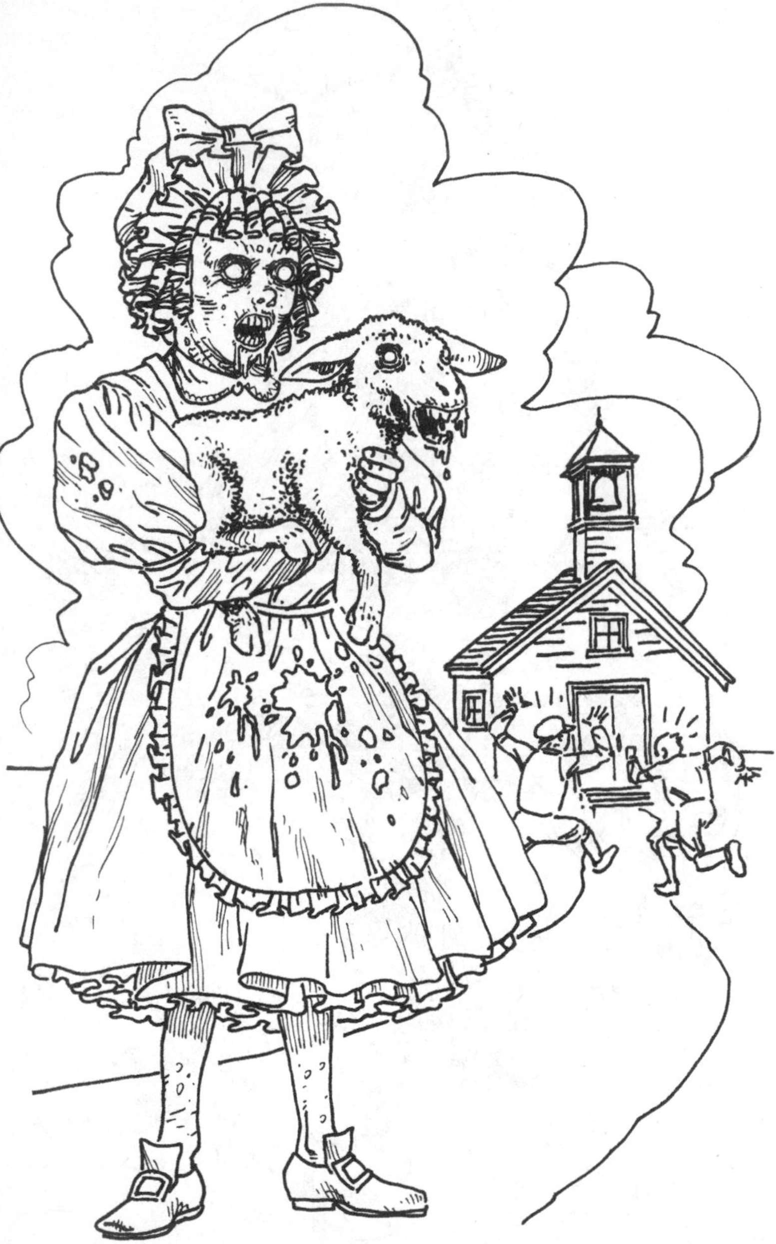

Mary Ran from a Zombie Lamb

Mary ran from a little lamb
It was Undead you know;
And everywhere that Mary went,
The lamb tried hard to go.
It followed her to school one day,
And tried to eat its fill;
It made the children scream and cry,
A Zombie lamb at school!

And so the teacher chopped it down,
But still it crept so near,
And lumbered patiently about till Mary did appear.
"Why does the lamb chase Mary so?"
The terrified children cried;
"Why, Mary has such tasty brains, you know,"
The teacher did reply.

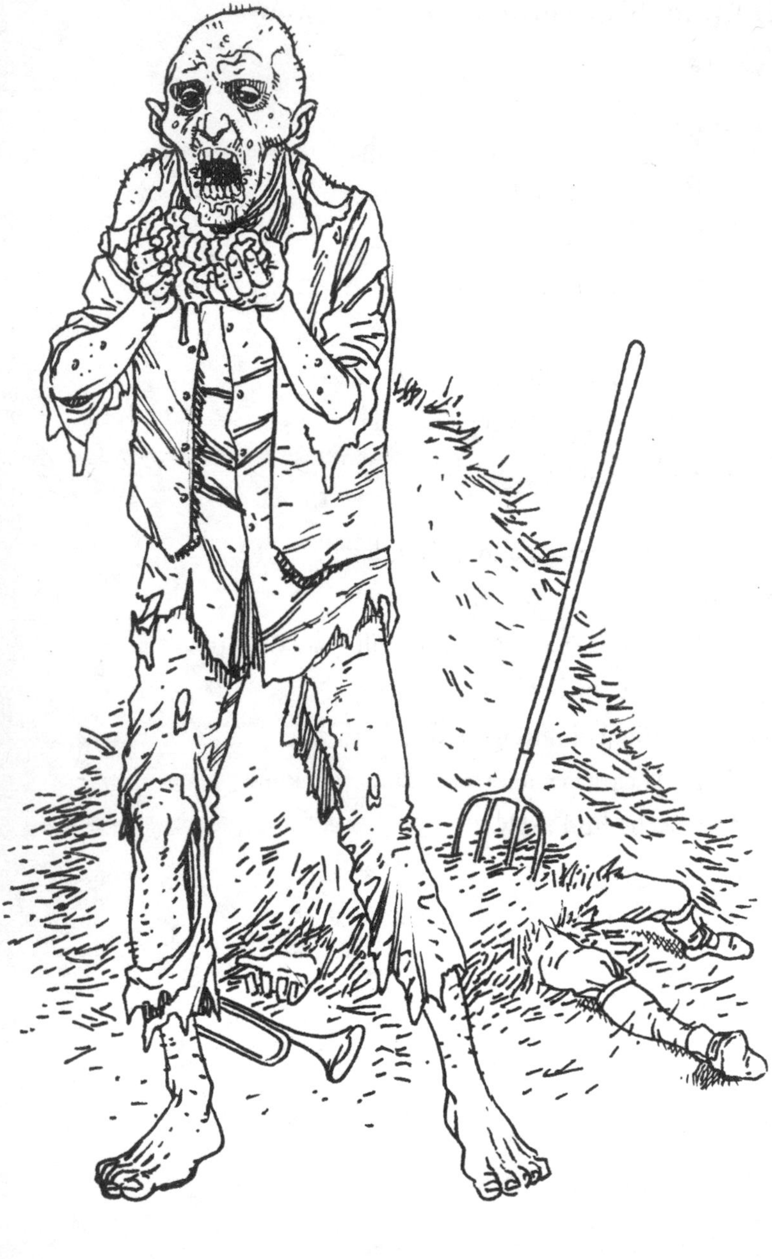

LITTLE BOY BLUE

Little Boy Blue!
  Come blow your horn!
A Zombie's in the meadow,
And the cow has turned!
A Zombie Boy
Ate all the sheep,
He's under a haystack,
Undead in a heap.
Will you wake him?
No, not I—
For if I do,
He'll make me die.

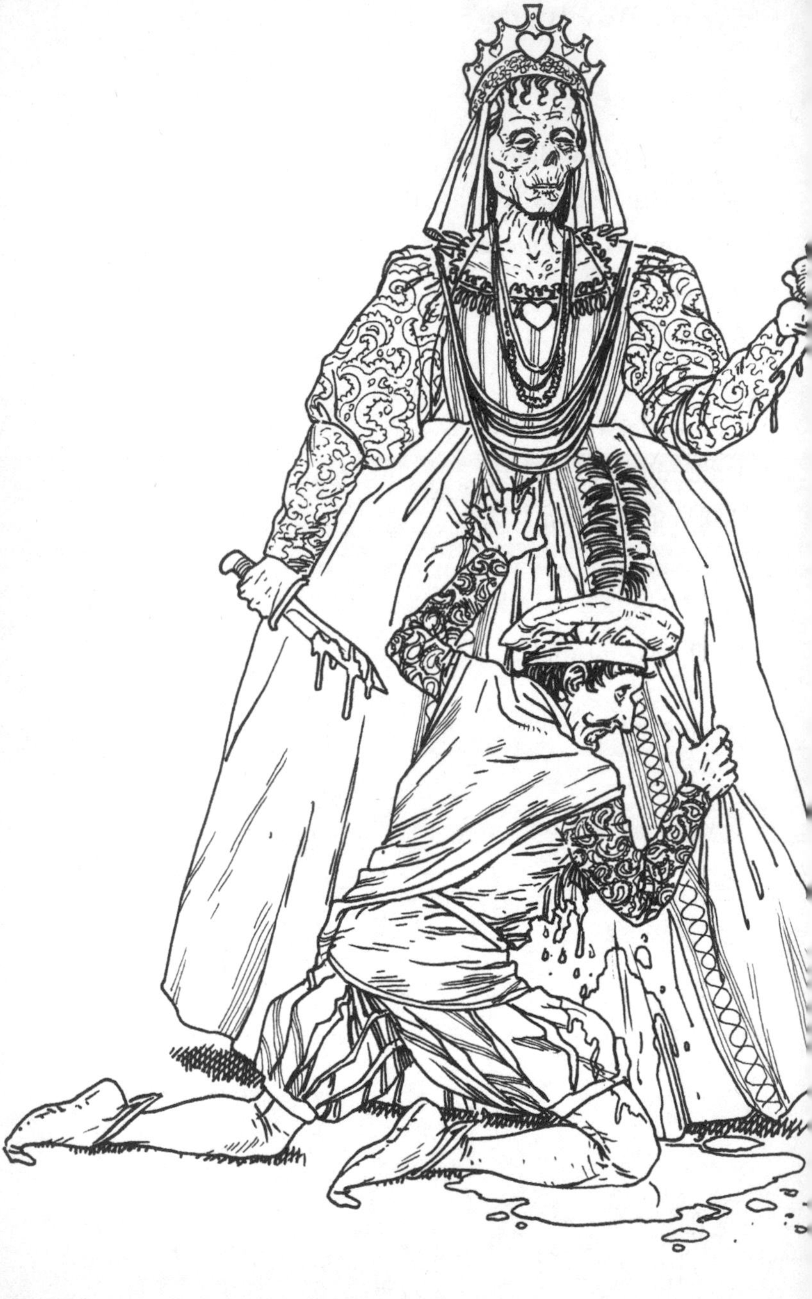

The Zombie Queen of Hearts

The Queen of Hearts she ate some parts
  All on a summer's day;
The Knave of Hearts he stole her parts
And took them clean away.
The King of Hearts called for more parts
And beat the Knave full sore.
The Knave of Hearts still ate the parts
And vowed he'd steal some more.

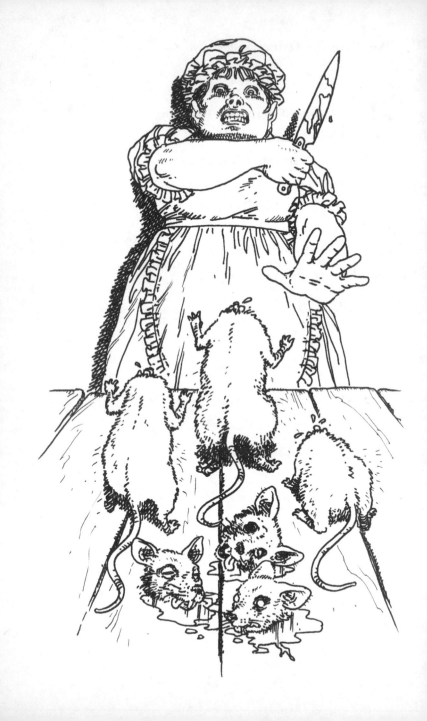

Three Zombie mice. Three Zombie mice.
See how they turn. See how they turn.
They all chased down the farmer's wife,
She tried smashing their heads with a big old knife,
Did you ever see such a sight in your life?
As three Zombie mice?

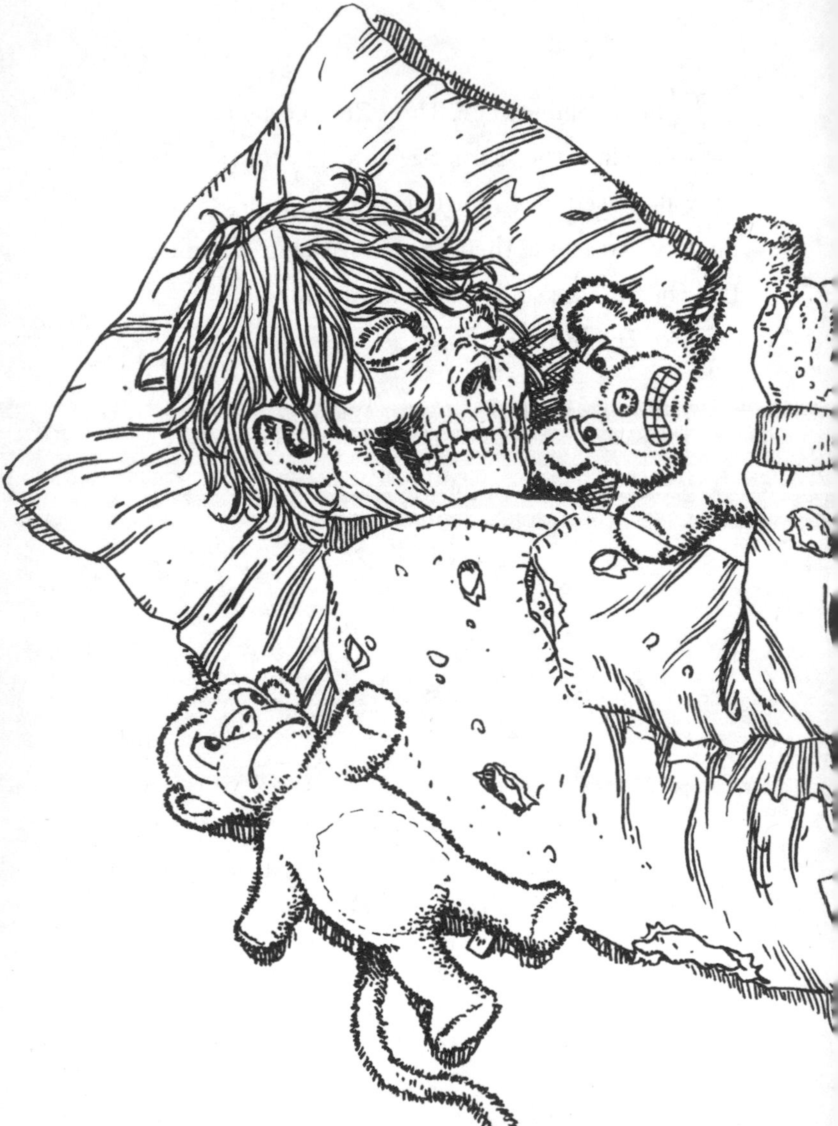

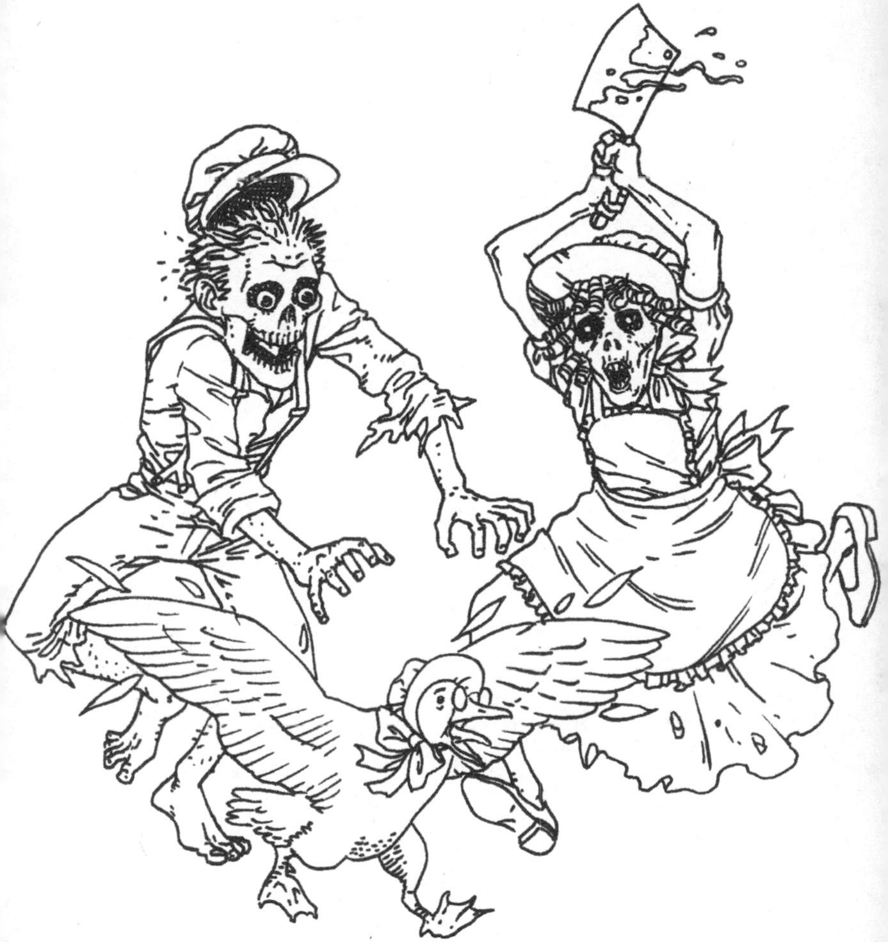

BOOKS BY MICHAEL P. SPRADLIN & ILLUSTRATED BY JEFF WEIGEL

Jack and Jill Went Up to Kill
A Book of Zombie Nursery Rhymes
MICHAEL P. SPRADLIN

JACK AND JILL WENT UP TO KILL

A Book of Zombie Nursery Rhymes

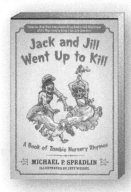

ISBN 978-0-06-208359-3 (paperback)

Spradlin and Weigel are back with more than 20 zombie-infused nursery rhymes like "Little Miss Muffet Turned on a Tuffet," "Three Undead Mice," "The Old Zombie Woman Who Lived in a Shoe," and "Jack Sprat was a Revenant."

It's Beginning to Look a Lot Like
ZOMBIES!
A Book of Zombie Christmas Carols
Michael P. Spradlin

IT'S BEGINNING TO LOOK A LOT LIKE ZOMBIES!

A Book of Zombie Christmas Carols

ISBN 978-0-06-195643-0 (paperback)

Spradlin and Weigel take over two dozen of our most beloved Christmas carols and shred them limb from limb, rewriting them from a zombie's point-of-view!

EVERY ZOMBIE EATS SOMEBODY SOMETIME
A BOOK OF ZOMBIE LOVE SONGS
MICHAEL P. SPRADLIN

EVERY ZOMBIE EATS SOMEBODY SOMETIME

A Book of Zombie Love Songs

ISBN 978-0-06-201182-4 (paperback)

A collection of over two dozen classic love songs aimed right at the rotting hearts of zombie romantics everywhere, with timeless tunes such as "I Want To Eat Your Hand" and "Tears of a Zombie Clown."